STEP UP TO IELTS

VANESSA JAKEMAN and **CLARE McDOWELL**

Self-Study Student's Book

CAMBRIDGE
UNIVERSITY PRESS

CAMBRIDGE
UNIVERSITY PRESS

University Printing House, Cambridge CB2 8BS, United Kingdom

Cambridge University Press is part of the University of Cambridge.

It furthers the University's mission by disseminating knowledge in the pursuit of education, learning and research at the highest international levels of excellence.

www.cambridge.org
Information on this title: www.cambridge.org/9780521532983

First published 2004
Reprinted 2016

Printed in Italy by Rotolito Lombarda S.p.A.

A catalogue record for this publication is available from the British Library

ISBN 978-0-521-53298-3 Self-study Student's Book
ISBN 978-0-521-53297-6 Student's Book
ISBN 978-0-521-53299-0 Personal Study Book
ISBN 978-0-521-53300-3 Personal Study Book with answers
ISBN 978-0-521-53301-0 Teacher's Book
ISBN 978-0-521-53303-4 Audio cassettes (2)
ISBN 978-0-521-54470-2 Audio CDs (2)
ISBN 978-0-521-53302-7 Self-study Pack

Cover design by Tim Elcock
Produced by Kamae Design, Oxford

Who is Step Up to IELTS for?

Step Up to IELTS has been written with two groups of students in mind. On the one hand, it is a short IELTS preparation course for use in the classroom with intermediate to upper-intermediate level students requiring a Band 5 to Band 6 in the Test. On the other hand, it could also be used by more advanced level students requiring fast familiarisation with the exam, as it covers all parts of the exam and presents authentic exam-level tasks. It is also just as useful for students studying on their own, who want to increase their language competence and IELTS test-taking strategies.

If you are studying alone we strongly recommend that you try and find a study partner with whom you can practise the Speaking material and some of the other partner activities, marked with the symbol 👀 in the book.

In addition to the core text, there is also a *Personal Study Book*, which provides supplementary exercises for extra class practice or homework. Together these form a comprehensive course, designed to lead you from a pre-IELTS level up to the realistic level of the Test.

How will *Step Up to IELTS* help me prepare for the Test?

Step Up to IELTS is highly focused on the IELTS Test – every activity is relevant to the Test and designed to help you with a specific aspect of the test. We recommend that you work your way systematically through the book to make the most of its progressive structure. If you want to vary this, however, you will find a comprehensive *Map of the Book* outlining the content of each unit, to allow you to select material as required.

An overview of the IELTS Test is given on page 141.

Special features of *Step Up to IELTS* are:

- The 16 units cover a range of topics that commonly occur in the IELTS Test so that you can build vocabulary and ideas related to these. The *Useful words* and *Useful expressions* boxes that appear throughout also help you with this.

- Practice is given in the range of IELTS question types and tasks that can be found in each of the modules: Listening, Reading, Writing, Speaking.

- *General Training Reading* and *Writing* modules are covered in addition to the *Academic* modules.

- A unique feature of the book is the *Step Up* activity in each unit, which gives you a step-by-step approach to IELTS question-types and tasks in each section of each module of the Test. These build test skills gradually, with shorter, lower level achievable test-type tasks for practice, leading to more challenging tasks at the authentic test level.

- *Language check* pages revise useful points of grammar. *Grammar boxes* throughout the book also focus on key language points.

- *Reading* pages encourage you to analyse the texts and understand the skills that are being tested and this will help you approach the questions in the Test more effectively. All the task types covered in the book relate to both the *Academic* and *General Training* modules.

- *Listening* and *Writing* pages build your competence in the specific skills required in these areas.

- *Speaking* pages cover all aspects of the interview, with ideas on how to approach the examiner's questions.

- You will find numerous *Test tips* on how to avoid losing marks through inaccuracies or failing to answer the questions correctly. The *Test tips* also offer advice on how to maximise your band score.

- The *Test practice* sections at the end of each unit are authentic IELTS-type test papers. They can be used to form a complete sample test.

- The *Personal Study Book* provides extra vocabulary, grammar and writing practice and makes an ideal supplementary text.

- The *With Answers* edition of the Student's Book includes a full key to all questions, including the IELTS Test Practice at the end of each unit, and there is a recording script for the listening sections, with the answers underlined. Sample Band 9 answers are provided for the Writing Tasks, as models of how to tackle these questions, but we would emphasise that these are only samples, and many other answers would be possible.

✓ **Remember**

When you enrol, you must decide whether to sit the Academic or the General Training version of the test. You cannot sit both at the same time. The two versions do not carry the same weight. Check the IELTS Handbook for details.

	Topic	Listening	Reading	Writing
UNIT 1	*Take a break*	Working out the topic Short-answer questions	Introduction to skimming and scanning	Introduction and tone of letters Salutations and endings of letters Opening and closing letters
UNIT 2	*What's on the menu?*	Working out the situation Short-answer questions	Skimming and scanning short extracts *Step up to* IELTS Short-answer questions and multiple matching	
UNIT 3	*On the road*	Understanding description *Step up to* IELTS Section 1 Form filling	Getting the gist *Step up to* IELTS Summary completion	Describing a process or diagram Organising the information into paragraphs
UNIT 4	*All at sea*		Skimming for main ideas *Step up to* IELTS Sentence completion	Analysing charts Describing diagrams and pictures Writing a paragraph
UNIT 5	*Come rain or shine*	Understanding opinions and reasons Note completion		Describing tables Using comparatives to describe trends and highlight details *Step up to* IELTS General Training Task 1
UNIT 6	*Value for money*	Identifying trends Multiple-choice graphs	Following a sequence of events *Step up to* IELTS Flow chart / note completion	Trends and verb tenses Describing a bar chart using the correct tense / verb form *Step up to* IELTS Academic Task 1 Describing a bar chart
UNIT 7	*Ignorance is bliss*		*Step up to* IELTS Paragraph headings	Forming ideas Brainstorming opposing ideas Writing paragraphs
UNIT 8	*Fit as a fiddle*	Listening for specific information *Step up to* IELTS Section 2		Describing the data using noun phrases
UNIT 9	*The driving force*		Recognising the structure of a passage *Step up to* IELTS True / False / Not Given Summary with box	Comparing data Describing bar charts Highlighting significant features

UNIT 10	*The silver screen*	Reading ahead
		Listening and note taking
			Dealing with longer passages
			Step up to IELTS Picking from a list
			   True / False / Not Given
			   Global multiple choice	

UNIT 11	*The written word*		Identifying main and supporting ideas in paragraphs Multiple-choice questions	Paragraph building

UNIT 12	*Down to Earth*	*Step up to* IELTS Section 3
		   Short-answer questions
		   Selecting words from a list
		   Matching
				Balancing your views

UNIT 13	*Safe as houses*	*Step up to* IELTS Section 4
		   Note completion
		   Picture multiple-choice questions
				Analysing the question
				Step up to IELTS Academic and
				   General Training Writing Task 2

UNIT 14	*On the face of it*	Recognising feelings and identifying views	Dealing with research-based texts Summary *Step up to* IELTS Matching people to statements	
UNIT 15	*As far as I can see*		Following the writer's argument *Step up to* IELTS Locating information in paragraphs	Referring back Checking an answer
UNIT 16	*Mother tongue*		Understanding the writer's views *Step up to* IELTS Yes / No / Not Given	Task 2: For and against Organising your answer Writing a complete answer

Speaking	Language / Grammar	IELTS Test practice
Introducing yourself Talking about your hobbies and interests *Step up to* IELTS Speaking Part 1	*go* and *play* Adverbs and expressions of frequency *-ing* and *-ed* adjectives *really*, *so*, *very*	READING General Training Section 1 Short-answer questions Matching information to paragraphs
Expressing likes and dislikes Using facial expression, intonation and word stress Giving a full answer	*too + for / to* *so / such ... that* Past continuous for change of plans	READING Academic Section 1 Sentence completion Multiple-choice questions Short-answer questions
	Use of the passive	LISTENING Section 1 Table and note completion
Expressing preferences	Comparative and superlative adjectives *while, whereas, on the other hand*	WRITING Academic Task 1 Describing a diagram
Expressing feeling – word and syllable stress Agreeing and disagreeing	Joining different ideas	WRITING General Training Task 1
	Tenses for Writing Task 1	WRITING Academic Task 1 Describing a graph and pie chart
Pronunciation check: *-ed* endings Talking for one minute	Narration and past tenses *used to +* infinitive	READING General Training Section 2 Sentence completion Paragraph headings
Step up to IELTS Speaking Part 2	*will / would* (conditionals 1 and 2) *can / could* Noun phrases	READING Academic Section 2 Paragraph headings Summary Short-answer questions
Expanding your answer – giving reasons Part 1 review	Linkers *so, because, because of, as, since* Superlative forms Linkers *also, as well, too, however, similarly*	LISTENING Section 2 Note and table completion
Expressing and justifying views Part 2 review	Tense revision Simple past, present perfect and present perfect continuous *as long as / provided that*	WRITING General Training Task 2 *(This is also a suitable practice for Academic Writing.)*
Step up to IELTS Speaking Part 3	Adverb formation and use	SPEAKING Test
Discussing abstract topics Pronunciation check: / pr / and / v /	*stop + -ing* *stop / prevent from + -ing*	LISTENING Section 3 Listing Table completion Short-answer questions
Comparing and contrasting Supporting a view Pronunciation check: contractions		WRITING Academic Task 2 *(This is also a suitable practice for General Training Writing.)*
Expressing feelings and opinions	*should / ought to*	SPEAKING Test
Talking about the future Predicting and speculating Pronunciation check: word stress	*this / these +* noun *such (a/an) +* noun	LISTENING Section 4 Labelling a diagram Note and diagram completion
Language quiz Expressing certainty or doubt Indirect statements	Indirect statements with *if* and *whether*	READING Academic Section 3 Yes / No / Not Given Classification Multiple-choice

UNIT 1 # *Take a break*

SPEAKING

Part 1: Introductions

At the start of the Speaking test, the examiner will ask you some questions about yourself.
First, you will have to give your name and tell the examiner where you come from.
Then you will have to talk about your home town or what you do.

 1 Find out where your partner comes from and why they are learning English.
Also, find out if they have any hobbies. Report your findings like this:

> **QUESTION STARTERS**
> Where do you … ?
> Why are you … ?
> What hobbies do you … ?

> *Roberto's Italian. He enjoys fishing and basketball.*

> *Ping comes from Beijing in China. She's learning English because she wants to go to London to study engineering.*

Talking about your hobbies and interests

After you have introduced yourself, the examiner will ask you some general questions about yourself.
These may include questions about your hobbies and interests.

2 Look at the pictures a–h and name the activities.

3 Decide which verb, *go* or *play*, goes with which activity. Can you explain why? Talk about how often you do each activity.
Example: *I usually **go** skiing in winter. I often **play** soccer with friends.*

4 Why can't you use *go* or *play* with activities i–n below? Name the activities.

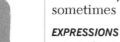

Useful words to express frequency	
ADVERBS	
never	often
rarely	usually
occasionally	frequently
sometimes	regularly
EXPRESSIONS	
every day/week/month	
once a week/month/year	
now and again	
from time to time	

 5 Say how often you do activities a–n and if you enjoy them or not.
Example: *I use the computer every evening. I really love it.*

-ing and *-ed* adjectives

1 **Complete the speech bubbles below.**

> *-ing* and *-ed* adjectives
>
> Adjectives ending in *-ing* are often used to describe something, e.g. This TV programme is *boring*.
> Adjectives ending in *-ed* are often used to say how you feel, e.g. I'm *bored*.

a It's amazing!

I'm _____!

b I'm tired!

This is _____!

2 **Complete the table of *-ing* and *-ed* adjectives opposite.**
Then use some of the words to complete the speech bubbles below.

	exhausted
boring	
	relaxed
satisfying	
	interested
	irritated
fascinating	
revolting	

a Professor Johnson is an _____ lecturer.

b This food is _____.

c I'm _____ by dinosaurs.

d I need a break. I'm _____.

e I'm afraid I'm not _____ with this new phone.

f It's _____ when you manage to find all the answers.

g Right now I'm watching TV. It's _____.

> You cannot use *very* with adjectives that already have an absolute meaning such as *fascinating* or *revolting*.

Using really, so *and* very

*You can add emphasis to your **-ed** and **-ing** adjectives by adding **really**, **so** or **very**.*

*Example: I was **really** bored. The film was **so** uninteresting.*

3 **Talk about which of the activities on page 6 you enjoy and which ones you don't enjoy. Try using some of the adjectives above with *very* and *really* to give a reason.**

Example:

Do you enjoy reading?

Yes, I do. I find it very relaxing.

Do you like playing computer games?

Not much. I find them really boring.

Working out the topic

In Section 1 of the Listening test, you will hear two people exchanging information on an everyday subject. The first thing you need to know when you do any listening exercise is what the talk or conversation is about. This is called the 'topic'. You will need to listen out for details and basic facts.

1 Which hobbies do these pictures show?

2 Make a list of the sports, games and hobbies that people in your class do or enjoy watching and the items or equipment that you use for these.

3 Look at the list a–j in exercise 4 below and write down all the words you know associated with each hobby or pastime. (Don't write on the table.)

4 Listen to seven short conversations. Decide what sport or hobby the speakers are talking about and write the number of each conversation in the appropriate box. There are more sports and hobbies listed here than you will need.

		conversation	clues	adjectives
a	Stamp collecting			
b	Running			
c	Chess			
d	Tennis	1	court, opponent, match, sets	exhausted
e	Football			
f	Water polo			
g	Gardening			
h	Fishing			
i	Surfing			
j	Reading			

5 Listen to the conversations again. In the column labelled *clues*, write the words that helped you to do the task.

6 Now listen again and make a note of all the *adjectives* which describe how the speakers themselves *feel* about the activities OR how they *describe* these activities.

7 Listen to a man on a radio programme talking about his hobby.

Answer the questions below using *no more than three words and/or a number* for each answer.

a Name one ordinary hobby that the interviewer mentions. ....

b What is the man's hobby? ....

c What is the minimum age to start learning? ....

d What does he most enjoy about it? ....

e What does he compare himself to? ....

Step up to IELTS SPEAKING PART 1

After you have introduced yourself in Part 1, the examiner will ask you some short questions about yourself based on different topics, for example, sport. Follow these steps to help you prepare for this.

Step 1

Ask and answer the following questions about sport. Practise using some of the words from the question to help you phrase your answer.

- What's your favourite sport?
- When did you first become interested in it?
- How often do you participate in this sport?
- What equipment do you need for this sport?
- Where do you do this sport?

Example: *My favourite sport is tennis/football/swimming.*
I first became interested in it when I was at school / last year.
I go/play every Sunday / once a week.
You don't need much equipment, just a racket / ball / pair of goggles.

As you listen, note any mistakes that your partner makes.
Give them some feedback and then swap over. Record yourselves, if you can.

 Test tip
It often helps to use the same verb tense as the question.

Step 2

*In Speaking Part 1 you may be asked negative questions, for example **What don't you enjoy?** Be prepared to give a negative answer. You can also try to vary your answers by including information about things you **don't** do.*

Think of a sport that you don't enjoy. Answer this question: *What don't you like about it?*

Think of three negative answers to this question: *What don't you do in your spare time?*
Example: *I don't usually watch TV in my spare time.*
I don't get up before 10 o'clock on my day off.

Step 3

When the examiner has finished asking questions about the first topic, he or she will move on to another general topic. Listen carefully so that you recognise the change in topic.

GRAMMAR

do not / don't + verb
I *don't go* to work on Saturday.
I *don't like* going on holiday on my own.

> Now, let's move on to talk about holidays ...   OR   Let's talk about shopping ...

Here are some more questions to work on. Make sure you give a full answer. You may begin your answer with the words *Yes* or *No* but you must say something *more* so that you show the examiner what you can say.

- Is there anything you don't like doing on holiday?
- Do you prefer to spend your holidays alone or with others? Why?
- What is your favourite holiday activity?

- How do you feel about going shopping?
- Do you like buying clothes or goods on the Internet? Why? / Why not?
- What don't you like about shopping?

 Test tip
Part 1 topics are always personal and familiar. Abstract topics are not discussed in this part of the test.

Step 4

Listen to the recording of a model Part 1 of the Speaking test.

Introduction to skimming and scanning

*Whether you are an Academic or a General Training candidate, you need to be able to **skim** and **scan** well in order to do the IELTS Reading test in one hour.*

*You can **scan** a text to get an idea of the topic or to locate a particular section. You do this by noticing the heading, pictures and the general layout. For example, you scan a newspaper to find an article you want. Once you have found it, you can **skim** the article to get an idea of what it is about.*

1 **Look at the pictures below and decide whether you would skim or scan in these situations.**

Is this the section of the library where I'd find English books?

Where is that Mozart CD?

What did the reviewer think of the film?

Am I free on Tuesday 10th July?

Are there any two-bedroom apartments for rent?

✔ *Test tip*

These skills will also help you in the Listening test, as you may have to quickly locate information in the question while you listen.

 2 **Take 30 seconds to skim each of these three texts and quickly answer the questions.**
  a What is the purpose of the text?
  b Who would read it?
  c What are the key words or features that help you decide?

MISSION TO SATURN

We are going to hear a great deal about Saturn and its rings and satellites when the spacecraft Cassini starts to orbit in July 2004. So why not prepare yourself with this excellent book on the history of the Solar System's second largest planet?

MISSION TO SATURN

SALE

2 pairs for the price of one $4.99

Offer this week only

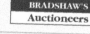

City Superstore

MODERN + CONTEMPORARY
Australian and International Art
Aboriginal Art and Artefacts

AUCTION
Tues 3 and Wed 4 December
6.30 pm

ON VIEW
Mon 2 December 11 am to 6 pm
25 King Street, Sydney

BRADSHAW'S
Auctioneers

3 **Take 30 seconds to scan the texts above to find the following information.**
  a the name of a spacecraft
  b the launch date of the spacecraft
  c the price of the socks
  d the day when you can see the works of art

WRITING

General Training Writing Task 1: Introduction and tone

In General Training Writing Task 1 you will have to write a letter in response to a given task.
The way you begin the first paragraph and the style you use will depend on:
- *the overall purpose of the letter*
- *the tone of the message you want to get across*
- *your relationship to the person receiving the letter.*

Test tip
Always bear in mind the reason you are writing your letter and who will read it. You will lose marks if you use the wrong tone.

1 Look at these opening sentences. Can you tell whether the writer knows the person receiving the letter? What is the purpose of these letters?

		Know the reader?	Purpose of the letter
a	Thanks so much for your letter and the lovely photos of the wedding, which are absolutely marvellous.	✓	To express thanks to a friend
b	I am a first-year student in the Faculty of Science. I am writing to ask permission to transfer from Biochemistry to Biology …		
c	I'm writing to thank you for your hospitality on Saturday. It was very kind of you to give us dinner even though we arrived unexpectedly.		
d	I am a resident at Flat 4, 43 Westbridge Road, Newport. I would like to report that a green Toyota van has been abandoned outside our block of flats …		
e	Following our telephone conversation, this is to confirm that, unfortunately, I will be unable to attend the meeting on 3rd March.		
f	On 15th March, I purchased a new car through your Perth showroom. Since then I have experienced a series of difficulties which I wish to outline …		

2 Which salutations and endings would you use with paragraphs a–f in exercise 1?

salutation	usage	sign off with
Dear Sir, Dear Sirs,	Use only when you are writing a formal or official letter and you do not know the person you are writing to, or their name.	Yours faithfully,
Dear Mr Smith, Dear Ms Park, Dear Dr Yong,	Use the title with the family name when you are writing a formal letter to someone you know or whose name you have been given. Use this salutation for people you don't know very well or where you need to show respect.	Kind regards, Yours sincerely,
Dear Rosemary, Dear Yoko,	Use given names only with people you know quite well. In business this is sometimes acceptable, but if in doubt, use the family name. Always use given names when writing an informal letter to a friend or relative.	Kind regards, Best wishes, Lots of love,

Opening and closing letters

3 Match the opening sentences a–e with the closing sentences i–v below.
Underline the key words that helped you to do this.

Opening sentences
a It was lovely to hear from you after all these years.
b I was really sorry to hear about Aunt Mary's accident.
c I am a student at your college and I am writing to ask a favour.
d Thank you for your letter regarding the position of office assistant.
e This is just to thank you for your marvellous hospitality last week.

Closing sentences
i Give my regards to your mother and best wishes for her speedy recovery.
ii I hope you are able to help me and I look forward to hearing from you soon.
iii I hope one day to be able to return the warm welcome.
iv We look forward to seeing you at the interview.
v Please stay in touch.

4 Match up the closing sentences in exercise 3 with the reasons for writing a letter.

> **REASONS FOR WRITING**
> 1 Giving advice
> 2 Apologising
> 3 Explaining
> 4 Requesting
> 5 Persuading
> 6 Complaining
> 7 Introducing yourself
> 8 Thanking
> 9 Suggesting
> 10 Expressing a feeling
> 11 Inviting

IELTS Test practice

GENERAL TRAINING READING Section 1

You are advised to spend 20 minutes on Questions 1–13.
First, read the texts below and answer Questions 1–7.

FITNESS FORUM

Open Mon–Sun 6.30 am–9.30 pm

CARDIOVASCULAR FITNESS
Daily aerobics classes
High Energy – Low Impact
8.00–9.00 am and 1.00–2.00 pm

STRENGTH & TONE
Walking machines – Weights – Exercise bikes
Booking advisable on weekends

STRETCH & RELAXATION
Yoga (Beginner to Advanced)
Monday and Wednesday evenings
6.30–8.00 pm

BADMINTON COMPETITION
Held every Tuesday evening at 6.30 pm
Individual tuition available from
Olympic coaches

For more information visit our website
www.fitfun.com.au

Reduced hours on public holidays. Enquire within

THE EDGE Climbing Centre

WHO? Beginners to advanced
WHAT? Casual visits / membership passes
School programmes a speciality
Corporate team building
Equipment hire
WHERE? 44 Clifton Hill Gardens, Clifton Hill
WHEN? Monday to Friday 11 am - 10 pm
Saturday 11 am - 5 pm
Tel: 9660 0968
WHY? The physical and mental challenge

Questions 1–7

*Answer the questions below using **NO MORE THAN THREE WORDS** for each answer.*

1 Which classes are offered twice a day?

2 How often are yoga classes offered?

3 Who trains badminton players?

4 When is the Fitness Forum not open all day?

5 What level of expertise do you need to join the Climbing Centre?

6 What does the Climbing Centre specialise in?

7 Where can you obtain the ropes and other items for climbing?

✓ **Test tip**

General Training Section 1 consists of short extracts and Section 2 has two parts. Only Section 3 of the GT paper is a long text.

Remember!

- Section 1 will always contain two or more passages.
- Texts are taken from advertisements, booklets, newspapers, timetables and other sources providing factual information for social survival.
- Here the task types are short-answer questions and matching, but in the Test you could get any task type in Section 1.

Approach

- Skim the texts to get an overall idea of what they are about. Use the illustrations to help you do this. Look for any common features linking the passages.
- Skim the questions and decide what sort of information is required, e.g. date/time.
- Scan the texts to locate the information.

IELTS Test practice

Questions 8–13

*The passage has six paragraphs labelled **A–F**. Which paragraph contains the following information?*

*Write the correct letter **A–F**.*
NB You may use any letter more than once.

8 the range of options offered by the AIS

9 the type of athletes who can attend the AIS

10 future guidance for AIS students

11 the effect the AIS has had on Australia's sporting achievements

12 the world-wide recognition of the AIS

13 the reason for establishing the AIS

 Test tip

You may see abbreviations of a name. These are always shown in brackets after the name the first time it is used. After this, they can be used on their own instead of the full name.

The Australian Institute of Sport (AIS)

A   The Australian Institute of Sport leads the development of elite sport in Australia. It has been highly successful and is regarded internationally as a model of best practice for the development of elite athletes.

B   The AIS was opened in Canberra by the Prime Minister of the day on Australia Day, 26 January 1981 and was initially established following the disappointing results achieved by the Australian team at the 1976 Montreal Olympics, with the aim of raising the standard of competitive sport in Australia.

C   The Institute made a significant contribution to Australia's tremendous efforts at the 2000 Sydney Olympic Games with 321 of the team of 620 athletes being current or former AIS scholarship holders. Of the record 58 medals that were won at the Sydney Olympics, 32 came from current or former Institute athletes.

D   The AIS operates nationally from Canberra, the capital of Australia, and is situated on a 65-hectare site there. It offers scholarships annually to about 700 athletes in 35 separate programs covering 26 sports, and employs around 65 coaches. Special scholarships are also available to Aboriginal people as well as athletes with disabilities and programs are located in most states as well as in Canberra.

E   The athletes who study at the AIS are provided with world-class training facilities, high-performance coaching, state-of-the-art equipment, a world-class sports medicine and sport science facility as well as accommodation for 350 residents on site. The AIS can also boast that it is at the leading edge of sport science and research developments through its Science and Sports Medicine division.

F   A national network of advisers helps athletes with career planning and personal development to make sure they plan for life after sport. The AIS also provides administrative, sport science and coaching services, as well as funding assistance to sporting organisations.

What's on the menu?

Skimming and scanning are 'enabling' skills as they help you answer many types of IELTS reading questions. It is important to practise these skills as often as possible.

To get going

  1 Take 10 seconds to *scan* all the headings in the article opposite. Then close your book and see how many you can remember. Tell your partner what they are.

 2 Take 1 minute to *scan* the article for the names of
a a country   b a royal person   c a flying insect   d a brand   e a fruit

  3 Take 30 seconds to *skim* the sub-heading and the beginning of each paragraph, then put your book down and tell your partner briefly what the whole article is about.

  4 Take 30 seconds to *skim* 'Brown or white?' then tell your partner briefly what it says.

Short-answer questions

*This type of question is common in IELTS. You have to answer in three words or less and the words **must come from the passage**.*

Step 1

Skim through questions 1–5 and underline the words that tell you what sort of information you must look for, e.g. the word *When* in question 1 suggests that you should look for a date. Scan the extracts for a date. What is it?

Step 2

 Take 3 minutes to answer questions 2–5.

Multiple matching

For these questions you only need to write the letter(s) on your answer sheet.

 Follow the steps above and take 10 minutes to scan the article opposite and answer questions 6–14.

IELTS READING TASK

Questions 1–5

*Choose **NO MORE THAN THREE WORDS** from the Reading Passage for each answer.*

1 <u>When</u> did Scott go to the South Pole?
2 How much fish do Norwegians eat in a year?
3 What colour are the shells of Leghorn eggs?
4 What type of injury did Scott's men suffer from?
5 What three important things does wholemeal bread contain?

Questions 6–14

*Look at the 8 extracts **A–H** about food.*

*Which extract mentions the following? Write the correct letter **A–H**.*

6 something that happened during a famous trip
7 the amounts of a certain food that are eaten by people from different countries
8 how the air affects a certain food item
9 a product that has a sweet taste
10 some research that took place
11 a belief that some people have about food

*Which **TWO** extracts mention the following?*

12 different types of the same food product
13 an unusual way of measuring what humans consume
14 more than one type of food

FOOD TRIVIA

Do you ever wonder why an apple goes brown if you leave it half eaten? Or why some eggs are brown and some are white? And why can't you taste garlic when you have a cold? Well, read on ...

A Brown or white?

Many people think that eggs with brown shells are better for you than those with white shells. Actually, there is no difference inside the egg, whatever the colour. The colour of the egg shell depends on the kind of hen that laid the egg. Rhode Island Reds, for instance, lay brown-shelled eggs, while Leghorns lay white-shelled eggs. All eggs are good for you, whatever the colour of their shells.

B A fishy story

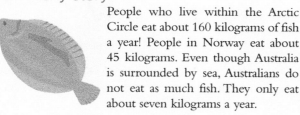

People who live within the Arctic Circle eat about 160 kilograms of fish a year! People in Norway eat about 45 kilograms. Even though Australia is surrounded by sea, Australians do not eat as much fish. They only eat about seven kilograms a year.

C Vitamin C

When Scott set off on his expedition to the South Pole in 1902, he took plenty of rations to stop his party becoming hungry, but forgot to take anything which provided vitamin C. The men developed frostbite because of the extremely cold weather, but the frostbite did not heal. It actually became much worse because they had no vitamin C in their diets.

D Beefing it up

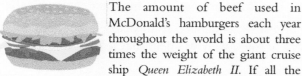

The amount of beef used in McDonald's hamburgers each year throughout the world is about three times the weight of the giant cruise ship *Queen Elizabeth II*. If all the hamburgers sold in the world each year were lined up end to end, they would go from the Earth to the moon and back more than 30 times.

E Sniff sniff

We can smell far more substances than we can taste. If you have a cold with a blocked nose, there are some foods which you cannot taste because you cannot smell them. For example, in a series of experiments, people were blindfolded and had their noses completely blocked. They were given coffee, chocolate and garlic, and had no idea what they were eating!

F Busy bees

Honey tastes nice to us but it is really a food for bees. For every kilogram of honey which is taken from commercial bee hives, about eight kilograms are used by the bees in the hive. The total distance a bee flies to gather enough nectar for the extra kilogram of honey taken by humans is equal to flying about six times round the earth. No wonder they are called 'busy little bees'!

G An apple a day ...

Apples (and lots of other fruit and vegetables) go brown once they are cut and exposed to the air. This is because they contain an enzyme which is affected by the oxygen in the air. It turns the flesh of the apple yellowy brown and then brown. If you brush the cut surface of an apple with lemon juice (which is acidic), the enzyme will not be able to work as well and the apple will not go brown for several hours.

H Bread

Wholemeal bread is made from the whole of the wheatgrain and is a light-brown colour. White bread is made from wheat which has some of the outer brown layers removed. Brown bread is somewhere in-between because it is made from a mixture of wholemeal and white flour. In some countries, colourings can be added to make bread look brown, but other countries do not permit any colourings to be added to bread. All bread is good for you but wholemeal is best of all because it has more fibre, more vitamins and more minerals than brown or white bread.

SPEAKING

Expressing likes and dislikes

In Parts 1 and 2 of the Speaking test, you will be expected to use English to talk about familiar topics. This will include talking about your likes and dislikes. In IELTS it is helpful if you look directly at the examiner and use your face to help you communicate. This is not considered impolite in English.

1 Ask and answer questions about your favourite / least favourite food. Report your findings like this:

Example: *Peter's **favourite** food is rice but he **can't stand** bananas.*
*Jane **loves** pasta but she **doesn't like** cake.*

> QUESTION STARTERS
> What's your favourite …?
> What food/drink don't you like?

I'm afraid I'm not very keen on pasta dishes.

✓ **Test tip**

good communicator   bad communicator

I don't like pasta dishes.

Useful words and phrases	
adore	delicious
love	tasty
not keen on	horrible
can't stand	revolting

Using intonation and word stress

Try to stress important words when you speak and use intonation appropriately. The Speaking examiner will mark you on your pronunciation of English as well as your use of vocabulary and grammar.

2 Listen to some people expressing negative feelings and underline the words that they stress.

I don't like vegetables and I really hate cabbage.

I'm afraid I can't stand cream or anything that's made with it.

Don't you think cold coffee's really horrible?

✓ **Test tip**

We often use *I'm afraid* or *unfortunately* before a negative comment. It is more polite to do this.

Practise saying sentences like these to your partner about food you dislike. Use facial expression to help you communicate.

3 Listen to people expressing positive feelings and underline the words that they stress. Notice the speakers' intonation.

I love eating vegetables, especially cabbage.

I really like cream and anything that's made with it.

I adore iced coffee – it's delicious.

Practise saying sentences like these about food you like. Use facial expression to help you communicate.

4 Sometimes we don't know how to explain why we like or dislike something. In this case it helps to stress certain words and refer simply to the food or the quality or effect that it has. Listen and practise saying some of these statements.

GRAMMAR

	type of food/drink
	meat/cheese.
I'm afraid I just **don't** like/eat … (at all)	**quality**
I (just) **can't stand** …	the smell of fish.
I (just) **love** …	the taste of ice cream.
I **hate** …	sweet things.
I (just) **really** like …	**effect**
	what toffee does to my teeth.

> You can use *just* to emphasise how strongly you feel and to show that you have no other reason.

Giving a full answer

You are not expected to give long replies to the examiner's questions in Part 1, but you should try to expand your answer a little and show the examiner what you can say.

5 **Categorise the adjectives in the box below according to what they describe. Some words may go in more than one category.**

bitter bland chewy creamy crunchy fatty fattening filling fizzy greasy hot juicy refreshing salty sickly sour spicy stodgy sweet tough	taste/flavour *bitter*
	the texture of food
	smell/aroma
	the effect food has on us

6 **Complete the sentences with an appropriate adjective from the box in exercise 5.**

a This is so .... that I seem to gain weight just looking at it!

b It tastes too .... cooked in all that oil.

c After a game of football I need a really .... drink.

d Wow, this curry's almost too .... for me.

e That was such a .... meal, I don't think I'll be hungry again for a while.

f I'm afraid .... drinks just make me sneeze.

g Ugh, this coffee is too .... Let's ask for a milder cup.

h They make these crisps so .... – then you drink more, of course.

> *too, so/such … that*
>
> The meal was *too* spicy for me (to eat).
> *too* + adjective + *for* + someone (*to* + verb)
>
> The meal was *so* spicy *that* I couldn't eat it.
> *so* + adjective + *that*
>
> It was *such* a spicy meal *that* I couldn't eat it.
> *such* + article + adjective + noun + *that*

7 **Ask each other questions about the food and drink below. Try to give additional information or a reason in your reply. Use intonation, word stress and facial expression to help you communicate.**

QUESTION STARTERS
Have you ever tried …?
How was it / were they?
What do/did you think of …?
How do/did you find …?

Useful adverbs	
too	pretty
terribly	fairly
very	quite
rather	

Example:

Have you ever tried noodles?

Yeah – I had them once from a take-away restaurant.

How did you find them?

Erm, I wasn't very keen on them. They were so salty that I couldn't finish them.

✓ **Test tip**
We often use the verb *find* to discuss our opinions on food.

LISTENING

Working out the situation

The IELTS Listening test has four sections. In each section you need to work out the topic, where the speakers are and what the situation is, as quickly as possible. This will help you answer the questions more easily.

1 Ask and answer these questions.

▶ When did you last eat a cooked meal?
▶ What did you have?
▶ Who cooked it?
▶ Where did you have it?

2 Listen to seven short conversations and decide where the speakers are. Write the number of each conversation in the appropriate box.

Listen to the conversations again. Write the words that help you decide where the speakers are in the column labelled *clues*.

		conversation	clues
a	Take-away restaurant		
b	Own kitchen		
c	Friend's house		
d	Outdoor barbecue		
e	College canteen		
f	Plane		
g	Restaurant	1	order, chefs

3 Listen to a young woman talking to a friend on the phone about a meal that she ate recently. Answer the questions as you listen.

a When did she go out to dinner?
b Who was with her?
c Where did they go?
d What did Martin eat?
e What did she eat for the first time?
f What did she drink?

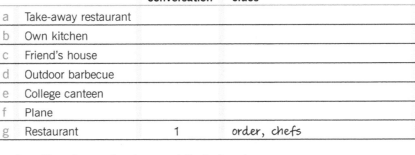

✓ *Test tip*

Sections 1 and 2 of the Listening test test your understanding of social/everyday situations, while Sections 3 and 4 have an educational context.

4 Listen again to the recording from exercise 3. As you listen, jot down all the verbs you hear. Then answer the questions.

a Which tense is used most? Why?
b Did they plan to go to the Italian café or the Japanese restaurant?
c What tense does the speaker use to talk about her plan?
d What tense does she use to talk about what happened after that?

5 Listen once more to the recording from exercise 3 and fill in the gaps below.

I .... them to my favourite Italian café … yes, the Napoli … but it was fully booked so we .... at the new Japanese restaurant.

6 Now think of three different situations in your life when you planned to do one thing, but eventually did something else. Work with a partner and tell him/her about these situations like this:

I was going to .... *but I ended up* .... *instead.*

IELTS Test practice

ACADEMIC READING Section 1

*You are advised to spend 20 minutes on **Questions 1–13** which are based on Reading Passage 1 below.*

Food for thought

Nowadays, you not only are what you eat; you R&D what you eat.*

To cajole nervous students into the chemistry laboratory, teachers used to say that the subject was like cooking. These days, it is truer to say that cooking is like chemistry. In a cut-throat market, food companies are unwilling to leave anything to chance. They must constantly formulate new flavours, ingredients and processing methods if they are to keep abreast of their competitiors.

As a result, their research laboratories have never been busier. A study published in November by a trade magazine showed that 42% of the 331 food manufacturers surveyed had plans to increase their R&D budgets by at least 15% in the coming year; only 3% said that their R&D budgets would drop. This money has spurred the development of new ideas in food technology.

To lower cost or improve texture, food manufacturers often have to replace one substance by another that tastes nothing like it. One popular substitution is soya protein for meat. In addition to being cheaper than meat, soya has (at least in America) the added advantage of being marketable. The country's Food and Drug Administration, which regulates such matters, has recently decided that if a foodstuff contains more than 6.25g of soya per serving, manufacturers can state on its label that eating soya may reduce the risk of heart disease.

That is a nice bonus. Unclogged arteries are not, however, the main point of eating hamburgers. Flavour is. So, to find out how far hamburgers can be 'extended' with soya, Keith Cadwallader of the University of Illinois at Urbana-Champaign analysed differences between the aromas of pure beef hamburgers and those containing 25% soya protein. Surprisingly (and gratifyingly), adding a bit of soya to a hamburger may actually improve its flavour. The mixed burgers had higher levels of certain sulphur-containing compounds that are believed to augment the meaty 'notes' in a burger's aroma.

On the other hand, the research of Margaret Hinds at Oklahoma State University shows what a fine line there is between temptation and disdain. Using a group of 81 untrained testers, she conducted a comparison of five commercially available burgers made from soya (and one made from beef, as a control). The hue, the firmness and the chewiness of the burgers correlated with how acceptable they were to consumers. Not surprisingly, consumers preferred burgers that had characteristics close to those of beef. Only one soya-based burger was close enough to pass muster.

Food, and its consumers, are notoriously subject to fads. This year, flavour makers are insisting that bolder tastes are in fashion. Frito-Lay, a snack-food maker, has recently launched a line of 'gourmet' crisps designed to appeal to the more discerning consumer. The company's laboratory started by generating 300 flavours, including Thai curry, blue cheese, lemongrass and tandoori chicken. Eight of these flavours made it to the final round and, after

*short for Research and Development (normally a company department)

IELTS Test practice

getting 400 consumers to sample them, Frito-Lay decided to mass-produce only four: cheddar and jalapeno; garlic and herb; barbecue; and something referred to as 'classic'. This quartet seemed to please the American palate most.

That sort of market research, though, is both time-consuming and expensive. It would speed things up, and probably cut costs, if it could be mechanised. To a certain extent, it can be. Cheddar cheese, coffee and tea researchers are all exploring the use of electronic noses to rate their foodstuffs. Simple versions of such devices employ a set of sensors made of special polymers linked to electrodes. The volatile compounds that make up an aroma cause these polymers to change shape, which alters the resistance to the current passing through the electrodes. The result is an electrical 'fingerprint' of an aroma.

So far, the electronic noses developed by firms such as Alpha MOS, of Toulouse, France, have worked best for quality-control purposes. These machines compare products' aroma-fingerprints with pre-programmed standards that are known to correspond with what people have said that they like. And the range of senses that can be substituted electronically has now been extended to include taste as well as smell. Recently, Alpha MOS has launched a second analyser – an electronic 'tongue' that can fingerprint the compounds dissolved in a sample of liquid. The machine is accurate enough to work out, for example, whether the vanilla extract in a sample originated in India or in Malaysia.

Even in culinary matters, however, the proof of the pudding is not always in the eating. The success of a food product also depends on the cleverness of its marketing. To this end McCormick, a flavouring company based in Maryland, has commissioned a 'craveability' study from Moskowitz and Jacobs, a market-research firm in White Plains, New York. The intention is to discover which descriptions of particular foods most induce craving in consumers. The preliminary results show that for fast-food hamburgers, the descriptions rated as most enticing were 'a grilled aroma that surrounds a thick burger on a toasted bun' and 'lots of grilled bacon and cheese covering on a lightly toasted bun'. Other blurbs, such as 'with horseradish sauce' and 'when it's cold outside and the burger is warm and inviting', actually put people off hamburgers. And that was before they knew what was in them.

Questions 1–3

Complete the sentences below with words taken from the reading passage.

*Use **NO MORE THAN TWO WORDS** for each answer.*

The writer compares food production to **1**... .

Two of the aspects of food production that are regularly updated by food companies are **2**.. and **3**.. .

Questions 4–8

*Choose the correct letter **A**, **B**, **C** or **D**.*

4 What did the trade magazine study show about research into food?

   A It costs more than it used to.

   B It is more important than it used to be.

   C It helps food manufacturers save money.

   D It is the most important area of food production.

IELTS Test practice

5 Keith Cadwallader's research indicated that people
   A welcome a healthier type of burger.
   B have become used to eating less meat.
   C cannot tell the difference between soya and meat.
   D prefer the smell of burgers that contain some soya.

6 Which aspect of burgers did Margaret Hinds ask her testers to compare?
   A their size
   B their texture
   C the benefits on health
   D the ingredients used

7 What does the writer say about Frito-Lay's new types of crisp?
   A Each type appeals to different people.
   B Each type includes a mix of flavours.
   C They have a more unusual taste than other crisps.
   D They have replaced other, less popular crisps.

8 The company McCormick are most interested in
   A ways of describing food.
   B popular types of food.
   C producing more hamburgers.
   D winning more customers.

Questions 9–13

Answer the questions below using **NO MORE THAN THREE WORDS** *for each answer.*

 9 What food products are being explored using an electronic nose?

10 Which quality of a food product does the nose respond to?

11 In which area of food production has Alpha MOS used electronic noses most successfully?

12 Which other mechanical aid has Alpha MOS developed?

13 What food product has been successfully tested using this aid?

Remember!
- You have to answer 40 questions on three reading passages in one hour.
- You only have 20 minutes for each passage so you need to use your skimming and scanning skills well.
- You will get a variety of question types in each reading section.

Approach
- Read the article and sub-heading to get a good idea of what the passage is about.
- For these three question types underline key words in the questions and scan for these or a similar word.
- Then read around the key words carefully to find the answer to the question.

LISTENING

Understanding description

Listening for detail is an essential skill. It enables you to answer questions based on numbers, colour or shape, and to differentiate one object from another.

 1 **Ask and answer these questions.**
  ▶ Do you agree with the saying 'Travel broadens the mind'?
  ▶ Do you enjoy travelling? Why? / Why not?
  ▶ Tell me about the best place you've ever visited.

 Test tip

In Part 2 of the Speaking test, you may be asked to describe an object or something that you own or would like to own.

2 **Look at the useful words in the box and label the different parts of this suitcase.**

Useful words

TYPES OF LUGGAGE
bag suitcase case
rucksack briefcase

MADE OF
leather canvas
plastic fabric

EXTRAS
handle strap wheels pocket
buckle zip name tag sticker

3 **Look at the luggage on the carousel below. Find examples of each of the following types of luggage:**
1 suitcase   2 rucksack   3 bag
4 briefcase   5 case

What sort of person might own each of these bags? What kind of trip do you think they have been on?

4 **Describe some of the bags to your partner. Use the words in the box without mentioning the colour. Did your partner know which bag you were describing?**
Example: *It's a small plastic case with a handle and a shoulder strap.*

5 **Do you have a travel bag? Say what it looks like.**

6 **Listen to the recording. You will hear six conversations. Decide which bag on the carousel the speakers are talking about in each conversation. Write the key words which help you to decide.**

	bag	key words
1	e	yellow, pocket, sleeping bag
2		
3		
4		
5		
6		

22

IELTS LISTENING *SECTION 1*

There are ten questions in each section of the Listening test. In Section 1, you will often have to answer questions that test your understanding of numbers, names and factual descriptions. It is important to be able to note these down quickly. Important names will be spelt for you on the recording. Remember that you will only hear the recording ONCE.

To get going

To practise writing names and numbers, ask your partner for the following information and write down the answers. If you cannot spell something, ask them to spell it out for you.

▶ today's date
▶ your partner's full name
▶ your partner's birthday
▶ an important phone number for your partner
▶ the name and date of an important festival in your partner's home country

Step 1

Take 1 minute to look at the Lost Luggage Claim Form and decide what kind of words you will need to listen for. Make a note of these in the far right column before you listen.

> **✔ Test tip**
> You will always hear an example first in Section 1.

IELTS LISTENING TASK

Questions 1–5

*Complete the form below. Write **NO MORE THAN THREE WORDS AND/OR A NUMBER** for each answer.*

LOST LUGGAGE CLAIM FORM

		type of word
Passenger's name	*Example* Dr/Mr/(Mrs)/Ms Mary Greenleaf	e.g. a name
Contact address	**1**	
Mobile	**2**	
Flight no.	**3**	
Coming from	**4**	
Date	**5**	
No. of items lost	two bags	

Step 2

Listen to someone who has lost some luggage and complete questions 1–5.

Step 3

Now look at questions 6–10 on the Description of Lost Property form below. Draw an arrow to show the direction in which you should read the form. Also, look at the headings on the form so that you know what you have to listen out for.

> **✔ Test tip**
> You should try to spell everything correctly. If you write a date wrongly (e.g. 22th November), you will lose marks.

DESCRIPTION OF LOST PROPERTY				
lost item	size	colour	made of	additional information
bag 1	**6**	blue	plastic	name inside and **7**
bag 2	medium sized	**8**	**9**	**10**

Step 4

Listen to the second part of the conversation and complete the form.

> **✔ Test tip**
> IELTS questions always follow the order in which you hear the information on the recording.

READING

MEKONG MAGIC

A JOURNEY UP THE MEKONG RIVER
By Brett Blanchard

By the time the Mekong River flows into the South China Sea, it has crossed six countries. In the process it has been worshipped, polluted, purified and used for legitimate as well as illegal commerce along the way. The Mekong has its beginnings in the Tibetan Himalayas and ends in the delta to the south of Ho Chi Minh City in Vietnam, which is where our journey began. We were headed first for a town called Can Tho, the biggest city in the delta area.

To get there, our car had to cross the Mekong at a place called Binh Minh, where a line of vehicles a kilometre long waited to squeeze on board one of four Scandinavian-built ferries. The river was perhaps 800 metres wide at this point and alive with traffic. On the advice of our driver, we decided to leave the car behind and cross on the first available ferry and then wait for the car on the other side.

We spent most of the 10-minute journey gently trying to avoid the people selling chewing gum, drinks, fruit and other snacks. The ferry docked on the outskirts of the town, and as there was no sign of the car, we set off for our hotel on foot.

In the morning, we headed off for Chau Doc, the last major town before the Cambodian border. The delta had once been part of the great Khmer Empire, and the last portion of Indochina to be incorporated into Vietnam. By mid morning the streets of every town were crammed with schoolchildren returning home – primary students in their white and blue uniforms, secondary schoolgirls in their elegant traditional Vietnamese costume riding bicycles in stately fashion. This was Teachers' Day throughout Vietnam, when students attend school to thank their teachers with presents and festivities and then head home again. The major effect was to produce a huge blue and white traffic jam.

Chau Doc appeared to be a model town. Situated among vividly coloured rice fields with the Sam Mountain in the background, it was the perfect market with the perfect produce in this amazing land.

Buddhism is one of the great religions of Vietnam and the Sam Mountain is a major pilgrimage centre. The road to the top of the mountain with its spectacular view over the fields to the Cambodian border is steep and winding, but always busy with pedestrians. We sat on the wall of a pavilion at the summit, 260 metres above the plain, and enjoyed the sunset over the flooded rice fields below, listening to the distant sounds of life from a village at the foot of the mountain.

When it was time to join the river again for the journey to Phnom Penh, there were only four passengers so instead of the leisurely ride I'd imagined, we climbed onto a speedboat and took our seats. At first we went slowly along the canals and there was time to enjoy the view of houses on stilts, sitting high and dry above the mud, but as soon as we entered the Mekong again, the driver turned up the speed. No matter how wide the river – and in places it was more than a kilometre – we rushed headlong towards any oncoming vessel and then, at the last moment, veered to one side or the other! We were all very relieved to reach the border post at Vinh Xuong, where we were able to disembark.

Getting the gist
It is important to do a quick read of the passage to get an overall idea of its content.

To get going

 1 **Discuss what you already know about the Mekong River.**
  ▶ Where is it?
  ▶ Which countries does it flow through?

First reading

 2 **Take 5 minutes to skim the text and answer these questions.**

  a Where would you find an article like this?
  b What is the main purpose of the article?
  c Who might read an article of this type?
  d What is the writer's overall impression of the Mekong delta?

Second reading

 3 **Take 3 minutes to scan the text for the following detail. The writer mentions five forms of 'transport'. What are they?**

IELTS READING *SUMMARY COMPLETION*

There are two types of summary question in the IELTS test. Sometimes you have to find the answers in the passage and sometimes you have a box of answers to choose from. (See page 66.)

✓ Test tip

Summaries often test your ability to find factual information in the passage.

✓ Test tip

In all IELTS reading tasks, it is always useful to skim the passage first to form some overall impressions about the article and why it was written. It is also helpful if you can identify the writer's view on the topic.

Step 1

⏱ **Take 5 minutes.**
Look at the handwritten notes in boxes which relate to the first two questions in the summary. Skim the passage on page 24 to find the answers to these first two questions.

Step 2

⏱ **Take 7 minutes.**
Now write a question in your own words for each of the remaining spaces 3 to 9.

Step 3

⏱ **Take 5 minutes.**
Re-read the passage to find the words which answer your new questions and complete the summary. You must use words which are in the original passage.

Step 4

Check your answers carefully.
- Have you spelt all the words correctly? Look in the passage to check.
- Have you used three words or less for each answer?

> **Where did his journey begin?**

IELTS READING TASK

Complete the summary below. Choose **NO MORE THAN THREE WORDS** *from the passage for each answer.*

> **How many countries does the river run through?**

SUMMARY

The Mekong River runs through **1** .... countries before it finally reaches the sea. The writer describes his journey up the river, starting out from the city of **2** .... in the south of Vietnam. At first, they went by **3** .... before catching a ferry across the river. From there they travelled **4** .... and spent the night in a hotel before heading out the next morning for Chau Doc.

The next day turned out to be a special day for **5** .... in Vietnam, so the town was full of **6** .... Not far from Chau Doc is the **7** ...., which is a major centre for Buddhist pilgrims. The view from the top of the mountain was **8** .... and they could see the Cambodian border in the distance. The last leg of their river journey proved quite frightening because of the **9** .... of the boat, so everyone was very relieved when they disembarked at Vinh Xuong.

WRITING

Academic Writing Task 1: Describing a process or diagram

In Academic Writing Task 1 you may be asked to describe a process or explain how something works based on a diagram. You should write clearly and divide your answer into short paragraphs.

1 Read the IELTS-type question opposite.

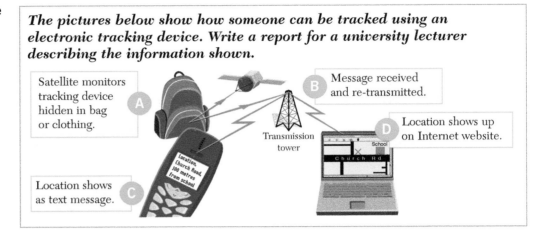

The pictures below show how someone can be tracked using an electronic tracking device. Write a report for a university lecturer describing the information shown.

Satellite monitors tracking device hidden in bag or clothing. **A**

B Message received and re-transmitted.

Transmission tower

D Location shows up on Internet website.

Location shows as text message. **C**

2 Think about how you will answer the question above. Decide how many stages the process includes.
Do you need a separate paragraph for each stage? Write an opening paragraph stating what the diagram is about. You should say:
  ▶ what the diagram illustrates
  ▶ how many stages there are in the process.

> ✓ **Test tip**
> You can use some of the words in the question, but do not copy word for word. Express the idea in a different way.

Use of the passive

The passive is commonly used when writing about a process or describing how something works, where the emphasis is on the subject or action, rather than on the person doing the action. For example:
The tracking device *is used* to locate missing people.
The messages *are transmitted* to a mobile phone.
The device *can be hidden* in a bag or a car.
This technology *has been adopted* by walkers and explorers.

Forming the passive
Verb *be* + past participle
Auxiliary or modal verb + *be* + past participle

3 Now write the rest of the answer using this framework and the Notes to help you.

> ✓ **Test tip**
> Remember you do not have to give an opinion in Task 1, but you do need to begin and end your writing appropriately.

PARAGRAPH 2
The first stage in the tracking process is to hide the device (the tracker) in an appropriate place such as a 1 ....
The location of the device 2 .... by satellite.

PARAGRAPH 3
A message 3 .... from the device to a
4 .... It is received and then
5 .... as a text message to a
6 .... indicating exactly where the person is.
His or her location can also be picked up on 7 ....
The device is able to provide details such as the name of the
8 .... or pinpoint a specific place on a 9 ....

PARAGRAPH 4
....
....

Notes
1 Look at picture A.
2 & 3 Use verb *to be* + past participle. OK to use the verbs in the diagram.
4 Look at picture B.
5 No need to repeat the verb *to be* here.
6 Use the information in picture C.
7, 8 & 9 Picture D can help.

PARAGRAPH 4
Sum up by saying something about the usefulness of such a device, based only on what you can see in the diagram.

IELTS Test practice

LISTENING Section 1

Questions 1–6

Complete the table using **NO MORE THAN THREE WORDS AND/OR A NUMBER** for each answer.

Hostel	Price	Facilities	Extras
East Coast Backpackers	**Example** Bunkhouse ......$5.90...... / night Cabins at $11.00 / night or **1** .... with air conditioning	5 minutes to beach **2**	**3** .... package
Emu Park Hostel	Weekly cost to share room **4**	Rooms overlooking beach have **5**	Good for **6** ....

Questions 7–10

Complete the notes using **NO MORE THAN THREE WORDS** for each answer.

East Coast Backpackers' Hostel address: **7** .... Road.

Bus will have words **8** .... written on the front.

Computer access costs **9** ....

Shop stocks things like **10** .... and ....

Remember!
- Listening Section 1 is always a dialogue. It may have two parts with a short break between these.
- The topic for Section 1 is social or general, with one speaker often seeking information from the other.
- The questions here are table completion and note completion, but there are other types of questions.
- There is always a sample answer at the start of Section 1.
- You will never need to write more than three words for each answer.

Approach
- Before the recording begins, read the questions carefully and try to predict the type of words you will need.
- You may be asked to spell a person's name or a place name in Section 1. You must do this accurately. Practise saying and writing the letters of the alphabet.
- Be aware of expressions such as 'double d' as in *middle* or 'capital S' as in *Singapore*.

All at sea

Expressing preferences

In any part of the Speaking test you may need to talk about or discuss your preferences.

1 Try saying this well known tongue twister:

'She sells sea shells on the sea shore.'

2 Ask and answer these questions.

 ▶ Do you live near the sea?
 ▶ How do you feel when you are near the sea?
 ▶ What do you like/dislike about the sea?
 ▶ Would you like to live on an island? Why? / Why not?

3 Look at the box of nouns opposite which are all related to the sea.

 ▶ Choose three words to be category headings. (The first is done for you.)
 ▶ Decide which category the remaining words belong to. Some words may fit into more than one. Look up any words you are not sure of. Make sure you can explain how you categorised the words.

BEACH
currents

beach boat captain cargo
currents dolphin lifeguard
lighthouse marine life
oceans octopus organisms
plankton rocks sailor salt
sand seaweed shark shell
ship shipping shore
tide wave

▶ *prefer*

When you use the verb *prefer* you can follow it with a *noun* or an *-ing* verb, e.g.

I prefer *bicycles* to *cars*.
I prefer *cycling* to *driving*.

4 Ask and answer questions about some of the topics below. Give a reason for your preference.
Example:

Which do you prefer – going to a beach or going to a swimming pool?

Oh, I prefer the beach. It's more exciting.

I prefer going to a swimming pool. I think it's safer and you can usually go all year round.

✔ **Test tip**

Try to give an extra piece of information in Part 1 of the Speaking test. But stay with the subject!

a a seaside or mountain holiday
b travelling by boat or plane
c an aquarium or a museum
d sharks or dolphins
e swimming in a river or the sea
f snorkelling or scuba-diving
g being by the sea or inland
h eating on the beach or in a restaurant

Skimming for main ideas

In the IELTS Reading test, you may be asked to recognise the main idea or ideas in a text.
You can do this by skimming the text quickly and forming a general overview of the ideas.

1 Take 20 seconds.
Run your eyes very quickly over this text. Then close your book. What do you think the text is about?
Where would you expect to find a text of this type?
How many words can you remember?

A ....

Most of our planet is covered by water. The great basins between the continents, in which all this water lies, are actually more varied than the surface of the land. The highest mountain on earth, Everest, would fit into the deepest part of the ocean with its peak a kilometre beneath the surface. On the other hand, the biggest mountains in the sea are so huge that they rise above the surface of the waters to form chains of islands.

B ....

The sea was first formed when the earth began to cool soon after its birth and hot water condensed on its surface. This early water was not pure, like rainwater, but contained significant quantities of chlorine, iodine and nitrogen, as well as other rarer substances. Since then, other ingredients have been added. As continental rocks weather and erode, they produce salts which are carried down to the sea by the rivers. So, over millions of years, the sea has been getting saltier and saltier.

C ....

Life first appeared in this chemically rich water some 3,500 million years ago. We know from fossils that the first organisms were simple, single-celled bacteria and algae. Organisms very like them still exist in the sea today and are the basis of all marine life. The biggest of them is about a millimetre across, the smallest about one-fiftieth of that. They exist in immense numbers – a cubic metre of sea water may contain 200,000 – and they drift in the water. These minute organisms are able to harness the energy of the sun to build the molecules which form their tissues. Among them float vast numbers of small animals which feed on them and which together are known simply as 'the plankton', a living soup which is the main diet of a multitude of other bigger creatures.

Extract from *The Living Planet* by David Attenborough

2 Take 2 minutes.
Read paragraph A again. Which of these facts is the main idea in this paragraph?
a The amount of water on planet Earth is increasing.
b Mountains under the sea are taller than those on dry land.
c Islands are the tops of underwater mountains.

3 Take 2 minutes.
Based on the main idea, but using your own words, write a heading for paragraph A.
Your heading should attempt to summarise what the paragraph is about.

4 Take 3 minutes each.
▶ Following the same procedure, decide on the main idea in paragraphs B and C.
▶ Write a heading for paragraphs B and C.
▶ Now think of a title for the whole text.

5 Compare what you have written with a partner. Decide on the most suitable title and the best paragraph headings for the three paragraphs.

6 Skim the text again and find a word or expression which has a similar meaning to these definitions.
a the top of a mountain
b animals
c large amounts (2 words)
d extremely small
e the outer face of something
f ancient remains of a living thing
g relating to the sea
h large areas of land

READING

IELTS READING *SENTENCE COMPLETION*

For this question type you need to skim the text to find the place where the information is located. You may also have to look for words which have a similar meaning to those used in the question. This is called paraphrase. Like in summary completion, you may have to find the answers in the passage or you may have a box of answers to choose from.

Step 1

- **Read question 1. The key words in the question have been underlined for you.**

- **Skim the first paragraph to find any similar words, structures or ideas. These have been underlined for you in the passage.**

- **Note how the contrast between the third and the fourth sentence in the text is represented by *but* in the paraphrase in question 1.**

Step 2

- **Follow the same procedure, underlining the key words in question 2 below.**

- **Find three words in the second paragraph which allow you to complete the paraphrase.**

Step 3

- **Take 10 minutes to do questions 3–7, which are based on the rest of the passage.**

IELTS READING TASK

Lighthouses occupy a special place in the history of modern Australia. They stand as monuments to the transformation of the nation from a colonial outpost to a prosperous society. For millions of people, lighthouses were the <u>first sign of civilisation</u> after a long sea voyage to a new home. For others, they are <u>grim reminders</u> of the sea's dangers. Modern technology has made many lighthouses redundant, but the buildings still evoke a special passion. They remind us of a time when ships ruled the world.

Lights for navigation have existed for more than 3,000 years. Their purpose has been to show ships where they are and to guide them into safe harbours or to warn them of rocks and reefs that could destroy them. Although preventing loss of life has always been a consideration, it is the preservation of ships and cargoes that has been the real driving force behind lighthouse construction.

Lighthouses evolved from a fire on a hilltop to towers engineered to withstand any force the sea could deliver, with beams of light that could be seen for 50km. They reached their zenith during the first half of the twentieth century but by the end of the same century their future had become uncertain. Today satellite navigation technology is taking the place of the lighthouse as the safe, economic and reliable way to navigate the oceans of the world.

The first primitive lights were fires in bronze baskets and were used along the Nile delta as early as 1000 BC. The oldest surviving lighthouse is the Tower of Hercules that stands on a hill on the north west coast of Spain. Built around 29 BC by the Romans, it served as a lighthouse until the fifth century AD when it was abandoned as the Romans left the area. It was relit by the Spanish in 1682 and has been in service ever since.

Italy's best-known lighthouse is in Genoa. Built during the 12th century, it was demolished in 1544 and rebuilt as a two-section brick tower. In 1449 one of the keepers was Antonio Columbus, uncle of the more famous Christopher. The light at Meloria, also in Italy and built in 1157, was the first rock or wave-washed lighthouse. Although it no longer exists, it was the forerunner to the many famous rock lighthouses of Brittany in France and of Great Britain.

The next challenge in lighthouse construction was to find a way to build towers in shallow waters on a sandy seabed. This was achieved with the development of pile lighthouses, made from either wood or iron with the piles being driven into the seabed. The first tower of this type was built in 1841 at the mouth of London's Thames River. But it was the USA which became the largest user of this type of lighthouse.

Accurate marine charts are now available for literally the whole of the earth's watery surface. These charts have also been computerised and in conjunction with GPS[1] can display the exact position of a ship on the screen. When connected to the controls of the ship it even allows the ship to be sailed on automatic pilot over any predetermined course in any kind of weather. The future is here.

[1] Global Positioning Systems

✓ Test tip

Don't try to guess the answer without finding the information in the text.

---

*Complete the sentences below with words taken from the reading passage. Use **NO MORE THAN THREE WORDS** for each answer.*

1 For people at sea, lighthouses are a <u>welcome sight</u> but also <u>remind</u> them of <u>the sea's dangers</u>

2 The real reason for constructing lighthouses is to protect ....

3 These days lighthouses are being replaced by ....

4 The oldest lighthouse still in operation is in ....

5 One of the former keepers of the lighthouse in Genoa was ....

6 The pile lighthouse was developed for construction on ....

7 Today's navigational systems rely on GPS and ....

✓ Test tip

Copy the answer correctly onto your answer sheet. You will be marked wrong if you copy words incorrectly or leave out part of the answer.

Making comparisons

Adjectives: comparatives and superlatives

- You add *-er* and *-est* to adjectives with only one syllable and to two-syllable adjectives ending in *-y*.
  *high – high**er** – the high**est***
  *happy – happ**ier** – the happ**iest***

  Negative adjectives ending in *-y* also have *-er* and *-est*.
  *unhappy – unhapp**ier** – the unhapp**iest***

  Some two-syllable adjectives with an unstressed final vowel and have *-er* and *-est* endings.
  *simple – simpl**er** – the simpl**est***

- You add *more* and *the most* (or *less* and *the least*) to all longer adjectives with three or more syllables.
  *prosperous – **more** prosperous – **the most** prosperous*
  *significant – **less** significant – **the least** significant*

- Common exceptions are *good – better – the best*
                        bad – worse – the worst

- You always need to use *the* with the superlative form.

while, whereas, on the other hand

We use these words to link ideas, facts and opinions that differ from each other.

While and *whereas* can come *before* the ideas or *between* them.
While has a similar meaning to *although*.
Whereas introduces a marked contrast.
On the other hand comes *between* the two ideas and forms part of a new sentence.

1 Go back to the text on page 29 and make a list of all the comparative and superlative adjectives used.

2 Complete the sentences by adding the correct form of the adjective in brackets. You may need to include *the* or *than*.

Example: The oceans are ……*deeper than*…… any river on earth. (deep)

a Electricity is one of …………………………………… discoveries of the last century. (significant)
b I like to do my shopping on the internet because it's …………………………………… than going
   to the shops, but it's …………………………………… . (convenient) (personal)
c Although it's …………………………………… to drive to work, I prefer
   to walk whenever possible. (quick)
d This is …………………………………… soup I have ever cooked. (spicy)
e Her English pronunciation has got …………………………………… and
   …………………………………… – she has almost no accent. (good)

3 Read the paragraph opposite and underline the expressions *while*, *whereas* and *on the other hand*.

4 Complete the sentences using *while*, *whereas* or *on the other hand*.

a …………………………………… Paris is famous for the Eiffel Tower,
   New York has its Statue of Liberty.
b Not all capital cities are the largest cities of the country.
   ……………………………………, it is unusual for a capital city not to
   have a population of at least a quarter of a million.
c …………………………………… Ottowa is the capital of Canada, it is by
   no means the largest Canadian city.
d I am interested in languages, …………………………………… my
   brother prefers mathematics and science.
e When I go to university I might study accounting. …………………………………… , I could do commerce,
   I suppose. I haven't really decided yet.
f …………………………………… lighthouses used to play an important role in maritime safety, they have now
   been superseded by satellites.
g Most bears are carnivores and eat meat, …………………………………… pandas only eat bamboo shoots.
h …………………………………… I can swim ten lengths of the pool, I find it quite tiring.

Sydney is famous for both its bridge and its Opera House. While the Sydney Harbour Bridge appears to be curved, it is actually made only of straight pieces of steel. On the other hand, the Opera House is designed to look like the sails of a ship on the harbour. Whereas the bridge has been there since 1932, the Opera House was not completed until 1973.

Academic Writing Task 1: Analysing charts

1 **Cover the charts on water usage below and see if you can guess the answers to these questions.**

a Do Australians use more water for cooking or for washing clothes?

b Do Australians use more water for washing themselves or for watering their gardens?

You will find the answers in the pie chart B below.

2 **Look at the charts below and answer these questions.**

a How is a bar chart (A) different from a pie chart (B)?

b In what way are these two charts related?

c What do the sections in the pie chart represent?

d If you were asked to summarise the information in these two charts, which of the charts would you describe first? Why?

e What, for you, is the significant piece of information in each chart?

Test tip

You will be marked on your ability to compare, contrast and organise the data. However, you should not interpret it or offer an opinion on the facts in front of you.

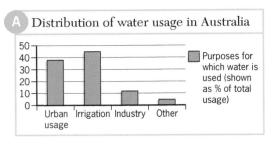

A Distribution of water usage in Australia

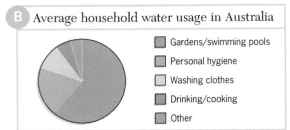

B Average household water usage in Australia

Useful words

amount
quantity
proportion
consumption
percentage
purposes
use
overview
breakdown

3 **Complete the writing below using no more than three words for each answer.**

> The two charts relate to different aspects of (a) ....
> in Australia. Chart A provides an overview of how water is used generally, whereas chart
> B gives a breakdown of (b) ....
>
> From the bar chart we can see that a slightly (c) .... percentage of water goes on
> (d) .... than on urban usage, 45 per cent in fact, while the proportion of water
> used in (e) ...., approximately 10 per cent, is far smaller than in either of these
> other areas.

4 **Now write another paragraph to complete the description of the data. Begin with the words**

From chart B we can see …

Describing diagrams and pictures

Remember, most Task 1 questions are based on a graph, chart or table, but sometimes you may be asked to describe a diagram.

5 **Look at the diagram opposite, which is known as a *cross section*. What does the diagram show?**

6 **Complete the paragraph below using no more than three words for each answer.**

The zones of the seashore

> The drawing provides a (a) .... of the different parts of the
> seashore illustrating the (b) .... tide marks. The area in between
> these is known as the (c) .... The area which is always
> (d) .... is called the subtidal zone and dry land in this diagram
> appears as (e) ....

IELTS Test practice

ACADEMIC WRITING Task 1

You should spend about 20 minutes on this task.

The diagrams below contain information about land and light penetration under the ocean.

Write a report for a university lecturer describing the information shown below.

You should write at least 150 words.

Profile across the sea coast of a continent (not to scale)

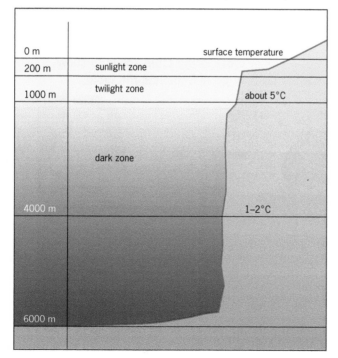

Depth zones of the ocean

Remember!
- In Academic Writing Task 1 you will always have to turn graphic information into written text.
- The information may not be presented as a graph or chart but may be a diagram or picture.
- The topic will be related to a field of study.
- There may be more than one diagram. If so, you should attempt to link the information in some way, i.e. comparing, contrasting, finding similar information.
- If the chart contains text, do not copy the phrases or sentences straight from the diagram into your report.
- If you do borrow any words from a diagram, make sure you spell them exactly as they are spelt in the diagram.

Approach
- Look at the diagrams or charts and consider the overall information they provide. Explain this.
- Look for any common features which link the two diagrams.
- Describe the information in a way which highlights the main ideas. Support these with some relevant details.
- Leave time at the end to check your answer for errors in grammar, spelling and punctuation.

Come rain or shine

Understanding opinions and reasons

In any part of the Listening test, the speaker may express feelings or views about the topic. Understanding these will help you answer the questions.

1 Ask and answer these questions.
- ▶ What is the worst weather experience you have ever had?
- ▶ What effect does the weather have on your mood?

2 Listen to four people speaking on a radio phone-in programme about the weather. As you listen, match the pictures (a–g) to the people you hear talking (callers 1–4). Write the letter in the second column of the table below.

caller	picture a–g	✓ likes the rain ✗ doesn't like the rain	main reason for this feeling
1 – Jane			
2 – Bruno			
3 – Mary			
4 – Liz			

3 Now listen to the recording from exercise 2 again. Put a tick or cross in the table above to show whether the callers like the weather or not. What reasons do they give? Complete the table.

4 Listen to the radio presenter asking his questions again and answer in your own words.

5 In pairs, practise the dialogue. One of you can be the radio presenter while the other is the caller. Ask and answer questions like the people on the radio.

In Section 2 of the Listening test, you will hear one speaker talking about a general or social topic.

6 Listen to someone talking about umbrellas and complete the notes. Don't use more than three words for any answer.

✓ **Test tip**

Note-taking is a common type of IELTS question. You may be asked to complete notes in any part of the test.

Notes

Umbrella – from the word 'umbra' meaning (a) ....

Used as protection against (b) ....

First Europeans with umbrellas (c) ....

16th century – umbrellas re-introduced in (d) ....

Showed a person's (e) ....

1850 – umbrellas made with a (f) ....

Umbrellas then became large enough for (g) ....

Expressing feeling – word and syllable stress

When we speak, we often express how we feel about things. We can do this by stressing certain words or syllables and by using words and expressions related to feeling. This is important in all three parts of the Speaking test.

1 **Say these words out loud stressing only the first syllable. Exaggerate the stress on this occasion.**

terrible **ter**ribly **mar**vellous **mar**vellously **des**perate **des**perately

2 **Now listen again to the speakers on the radio programme and repeat what they say. The words and syllables to stress are in bold. Don't stress the other words – they are weak sounds here.**

It's **great**.   I **love** the **rain**.
It's **ter**rible.   It's **dri**ving me **mad**.
It's **mar**vellous.   We **des**perately **nee**ded the **rain**.
I can't **stand** it.   I **much** pre**fer** the **sun**shine.
I **could**n't use an um**brell**a.   You look so **stu**pid carrying an um**brell**a.

> ✔ *Test tip*
>
> The way you say a word in English will depend on its position in the sentence and the meaning you want to give.

Agreeing and disagreeing

3 **In pairs first say how *you* feel about what is shown in the pictures below and then ask your partner for their view. Use intonation, word stress and facial expression to help you communicate. Try to give additional information or a reason in your reply. Use the expressions on this page, or go back to Unit 2 page 16 for some other ideas.**

Example:

*I **love** going to the beach. How do **you** feel about spending the day at the beach?*
*I agree. I **really** love being out in the sun. It's **great**!*
OR
*Personally, I **much** prefer to stay indoors. In my country it's too **hot** to spend all day in the sun.*

a day at the beach

travelling in the rush hour

cooking

women playing soccer

breaking the speed limit

Quiet
Exam in Progress

sitting exams

Useful expressions

AGREEING
I agree.
Yes, I really …
Absolutely. I …
On the whole …
Yes, me too.

DISAGREEING
I don't really know.
I'm not so sure.
Personally, I tend to think …
Um … I actually think …
Possibly, but …

> ✔ *Test tip*
>
> In order not to appear rude, we tend to be less emphatic when we express disagreement than when we agree with someone.

Academic Writing Task 1: Describing tables

1 **Look at the two tables below and answer these questions about them.**

  a What is the purpose of the tables?

  b What do you notice about the layout of the tables?

  c How do these tables differ from a bar chart or a pie chart?

Average yearly temperatures and rainfall for
Brisbane and Melbourne in Australia

Brisbane climate	Jan	April	July	Oct
Max °C	29	27	21	26
Min °C	21	17	11	16
Rainfall mm	169	86	66	102
Rainy days	14	11	7	10

Melbourne climate	Jan	April	July	Oct
Max °C	26	20	13	20
Min °C	14	11	4	9
Rainfall mm	48	57	49	67
Rainy days	8	12	15	14

✔ *Test tip*

Take a minute to absorb the information in the tables.

Do not begin writing your answer until you have understood the content of the tables as a whole.

Making sense of the information

2 **Examine the data by first looking at the overall trends.**
Make four statements about the information in the tables, using comparative adjectives.

> drier   wetter   hotter   colder   warmer   cooler

Example: *Brisbane has a hotter, wetter climate than Melbourne.*

3 **Now complete the sentences below to make some superlative statements about the information in the tables and then write two more statements of your own, based on this model.**

✔ *Test tip*

Note how the word *month* has been replaced. It is important to vary the words you use when describing this kind of information or your writing will become very repetitive.

Max °C	The hottest month in Brisbane is .... *January.* ....
	(a) In Melbourne ....
Min °C	(b) The coolest time of year in Melbourne is ....
	(c) July is the coolest ....
Rainfall mm	(d) The wettest period in Brisbane is ....
	(e) The driest period in Melbourne is ....
Rainy days	(f) Melbourne has the .... number of rainy days in January.
	(g) Brisbane has .... in January and the least rainy days in July.

Including relevant data

So far you have only described the overall climate patterns, without mentioning any specific details (e.g. temperatures or the number of days). However, it is important to include some of the data from the tables to illustrate the major trends. It is also important not to overdo this by including too much.

4 **Look at the example sentence in exercise 3 and circle the relevant information in the table.**
Read this example and note how the data has been included.

Example: *The hottest month in Brisbane is January, when the average maximum temperature rises to 29°C.*

Re-write sentences a–g in exercise 3 above to include the relevant data from the tables.
You can add the supporting data in a separate sentence if necessary.

Joining two different ideas

When data is presented in two similar tables, it is useful to focus on information which can be compared or contrasted. To do this, you need to join your ideas.

You can join ideas within one sentence using a conjunction. Alternatively, you can put each idea in its own sentence and join these with a linking expression.

5 **Look at these examples which compare information from the two tables. Note how the two contrasting pieces of information are linked.**

> The highest average temperature in Brisbane in summer is 29 °C, whereas the Melbourne maximum is only 26 °C.

Single sentence: ideas linked by a conjunction – 'whereas'.

> The highest average temperature in Brisbane in summer is 29 °C. By contrast, the Melbourne maximum is only 26 °C.

Information given in two sentences: ideas linked by a word or phrase.

6 **Expand the following notes to make sentences. Use conjunctions or linking expressions from the boxes.**

a   more rainy days – July – Melbourne than Brisbane / January – Brisbane wetter than Melbourne

b   October wettest month Melbourne – January wettest month Brisbane / both average 14 rainy days

c   July coldest month Brisbane and Melbourne / maximum temperatures higher Brisbane than Melbourne

d   January rainfall Brisbane – greater than Melbourne / six more days of rain

e   difference of 8 °C – maximum and minimum temperatures – Brisbane – summer / Melbourne difference larger / difference decreases in winter – July

Useful conjunctions

whereas   but   except that   compared with
while   although   even though

Useful expressions for introducing an opposite idea in a new sentence

On the other hand …
Nevertheless …
However …
By contrast …
All the same …
Alternatively …

Writing a paragraph

7 **Complete the paragraph below on temperature.**
Note how this paragraph includes two actual pieces of data.

> Brisbane and Melbourne have similar climates. However, we can see from the information provided that Brisbane is (a) .... than Melbourne although the differences in (b) .... are not huge. One interesting point is that the temperature in Brisbane never drops below (c) ...., even in winter in July. Melbourne, on the other hand, experiences (d) .... winters with average minimum temperatures as low as 4 °C.

 ✔ *Test tip*

It is important to make sure that the information you choose to describe is accurate. If you make statements which are not factually correct, you may lose marks.

8 **Using the paragraph above as a model, write a paragraph comparing the average rainfall in the two cities. Start with a clear statement to introduce the topic. Then write at least two more sentences highlighting some of the information.**

Step up to IELTS GENERAL TRAINING WRITING *TASK 1*

In General Training Writing Task 1 you will have to write a letter of 150 words. You must cover all three of the bullet points in your letter and begin and end your letter appropriately. You also need to write in paragraphs and use the right tone.

Step 1

Read the task opposite and decide what type of letter is required, e.g. formal or informal, and what the purpose of the letter is. Underline the key words that help you decide.

> *You have recently heard that a friend of yours has had some problems as a result of some unusual weather. Write a letter to your friend.*
> *In your letter*
> - *express concern (i.e. say you are sorry to hear what has happened)*
> - *tell them about a similar experience that you once had*
> - *give some advice or offer help.*

Step 2

Brainstorm some ideas about unusual weather and the damage it can cause. Complete the table to help you and note any other useful vocabulary.

types of weather	useful words	possible damage
	storm / gale	roof blown off house
wet	flood	
	fires	
dry	drought	
cold	ice / snow	

Step 3

Complete the following notes with some ideas and words that you could use in your letter. You have to write at least 150 words so you need to use your imagination.

- Shocked to hear about the (a) .... and damage to (b) .... – very (c) ....
- Understand the feeling of (d) ....
  Our house once (e) ....
  Insurance covered cost of (f) ....
  – now fully repaired
- Think positively:
  opportunity to (g) ....
  happy to help (h) ....
- Closing ideas (i) ....

✓ **Test tip**

Note how the three bullet points help you organise your letter into clear paragraphs.

Step 4

Take 15 minutes.
Expand the notes into a complete letter. Remember you are writing to a friend, so the letter can be quite informal and friendly in style. You could use the expressions in the boxes or go back to Unit 1 for some more ideas on ways to begin and end letters.

Step 5

Read your letter carefully to check the grammar, spelling and organisation.

Summary

Remember to follow these steps when you do Writing Task 1.
- **Brainstorm ideas for what to say.**
- **Note useful vocabulary.**
- **Make notes for each paragraph.**
- **Expand your notes into a letter.**
- **Check your letter carefully.**

Useful expressions of concern

I was very sorry to hear about …
I'm sorry to learn about …
I was shocked by the news that …
I was concerned/upset to hear that …

NB Do not say 'What a pity!' when the situation is really serious.

Useful expressions for offering help

Let me know if I can …
Don't hesitate to get in touch if you need …
I hope things work out all right.

IELTS Test practice

GENERAL TRAINING WRITING Task 1

You should spend about 20 minutes on this task.

You recently stayed in a hotel in a large city. The weather was very unusual for the time of year and the heating/cooling system in the hotel was quite inadequate.

Write a letter to the manager of the hotel. In your letter

- *give details of what was wrong*
- *explain what you had to do to overcome the problem at the time*
- *say what action you would like the manager to take.*

You should write at least 150 words.

You do NOT need to write your own address.

Begin your letter as follows:

Dear .... ,

 Test tip

If you do not write something about each point you will lose marks.

Remember!

- In GT Writing Task 1 you will always have to write a letter. You will be given a situation and three main points which you must write about.
- The letter may be to someone you know, such as a friend or a teacher, or it may be a formal letter to a stranger or an official.
- The style you choose, and the opening and closing sentences, will depend on your relationship to this person.
- The letter will have a particular purpose such as thanking someone / asking someone to do something / complaining / requesting information / asking for a favour / offering to help someone.
- You should take 20 minutes for this. There are two tasks in the Writing test and Task 2 carries more marks. So it is important to stick to the time limit suggested for Task 1.

Approach

- Read the question carefully to make sure you have fully understood the function of the letter, i.e. the reason for writing it.
- Look at the three points and think of something to write about each of them.
- Write a plan along the lines of the notes you wrote earlier in this unit.
- Expand your plan into a full answer.
- Leave time at the end to check your answer for errors in grammar, spelling and punctuation.

Value for money

Following a sequence of events

Some IELTS passages give a historical account of something as it happened over time.
Recognising this type of passage will help you develop a mental picture of the overall content.

First reading

Look at the list of useful nouns which are all connected to money and the economy. Look up any words you don't know in a good dictionary. Read the article and choose a noun from the list to fill each gap, using the sentence to help you work out the meaning.

Useful nouns		
paper money	account	prices
bill	banknotes	currency
value	exchange	inflation
change	trade	

Paper Money

January 1st 2002 saw the biggest ever introduction of new banknotes on a single day. It went smoothly – but the history of paper money is littered with warnings.

In the last few months of 2001, 14 billion brand new banknotes, ranging in (a) .... from 500 euros down to 5 euros, were printed by the 12 countries that adopted Europe's single (b) .... Old money continued to circulate for four to eight weeks afterwards, depending on the country, but department stores and supermarkets quickly made the change to the euro.

The search for a means of (c) .... is almost as old as mankind. Among the commodities that have been tried are chocolate (the Aztecs), shells (Pacific Islanders), butter and salt (from which the word 'salary' was derived). In Europe after the Second World War cigarettes were used, and in Italy it was common as late as the 1970s to use sweets as small (d) ....

The idea of using paper as money is almost as old as paper itself. The first people to do it were the Chinese, who made the earliest banknotes over 1,000 years ago. However, they soon grew so fond of their invention that they printed far too much and this led to (e) .... The most famous issuer of paper money was Kublai Khan, the Mongol who ruled the Chinese empire in the 13th century. Kublai Khan also confiscated all gold and silver, even if it was brought in through foreign (f) ....

Though explorers like Marco Polo were impressed with the Chinese system, paper money did not succeed everywhere. In Persia, its introduction led to a total collapse of trade. By the 15th century even China had more or less given up on paper money.

In Europe, the first issuer of paper money was Sweden. In 1661, Johan Palmstruch's Stockholm Banco introduced the first banknotes. Other European countries soon followed the Swedish lead. One reason for establishing the Bank of England in 1694 was to print paper money so that the balance could be kept in a bank (g) .... The bank is now the longest continuous issuer of banknotes in the world. In France, the Banque Royale was set up in 1718. It was very successful at first, but when people realised that it had issued twice as much (h) .... as France's total supply of gold and silver, confidence went and the bank collapsed. Nowadays, national banks realise that the quantity of paper money they issue has to be regulated.

The real masters of paper money, however, were across the Atlantic in America. And the father of American paper currency is undoubtedly Benjamin Franklin, the man who features on today's hundred dollar (i) .... He was a printer who strongly believed in the benefits of paper money.

So who has the best banknotes? Almost everybody would agree that America's should be at or near the bottom. Top position depends, naturally, on taste, although it is often the smaller countries, such as Guatemala, that print the most attractive notes. In Europe, some experts praise the modern designs of countries such as the Netherlands and Finland. Australia is a pioneer in the use of plastic, rather than paper. Over the past decade, most of the countries of Eastern Europe and the ex-Soviet Union have chosen to introduce new (j) .... The most attractive are said to be Estonia's and Macedonia's.

However, the best notes of all are, in many ways, those not printed by central banks at all. For years, the Hong Kong and Shanghai Banking Company acted as the city's central bank. Even today, its notes are much admired. In the collector's market old Hong Kong Bank notes fetch exceptionally high (k) .... – one note from 1867 was sold in London recently for £85,000.

IELTS READING *FLOW CHART / NOTE COMPLETION*

Completing a flow chart or set of notes is not very different from completing a summary (see Unit 3). In a flow chart, the arrows indicate the links between points. Notes may be presented using bullets.

Step 1

Look at the notes and questions opposite and decide whether they test the whole passage or a section of the passage. If they test a section, skim in order to find the right section.

Step 2

Decide what sort of factual information you need to find for each question (e.g. a person or country). Turn the notes into questions using words like *What*, *Where* and *When*.

Step 3

Take 8 minutes to answer questions 1–6 opposite.

- **Look at the words in the notes and think of similar words that might appear in a sentence in the text.**

- **Scan the text to see if any of the words in the notes, or similar words that you have identified, jump out at you.**

- **Read those sentences more closely to see if the answer you need is there.**

- **Write down your answer and make sure it is no longer than three words and is spelt correctly.**

Each IELTS reading passage has 13 or 14 questions but they will not all be of the same type. Here are some more questions on this passage.

IELTS READING TASK

Complete the notes using **NO MORE THAN THREE WORDS** *from the reading passage.*

History of paper money

Ancient forms of money: e.g. ......chocolate......
1 .... and ....

▼

First banknotes printed by **2** ....
(10th century)

▼

Over production of paper money

▼

13th century – most famous producer of banknotes:
3 ....

▼

First European banknotes issued in **4** ....

▼

1694 – bank accounts set up by the **5** ....

▼

Most recent form of currency **6** ....

[annotation, pointing to "Ancient":] Means 'old'. Scan for both words.

 Test tip

You will lose marks if you use more than three words for summary, sentence or note completion questions or if you spell the answers incorrectly.

Step 4

Take 5 minutes to do this set of note-completion questions. Follow step 3 and check the length and spelling of your answers.

IELTS READING TASK

Complete the notes below. Choose **NO MORE THAN THREE WORDS** *from the passage for each answer.*

- In 2001, **7** .... euro banknotes were printed.
- A total of **8** .... countries agreed to use the euro.
- Kublai Khan prevented people from trading in **9** .... and ....
- Benjamin Franklin worked as a **10** ....
- The prettiest banknotes are often produced by **11** ....
- Notes made from a substance other than paper are used in **12** ....
- Banknotes from **13** .... are very popular among collectors.

Unit 6 **Value for money**

Identifying trends

In the Writing test, you may have to describe the trends on a graph. Also, in the Listening test (usually Section 3 or 4), you may have to identify trends in a multiple-choice or labelling task.

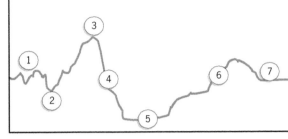

What happened to share prices?

1 Match the numbered parts of the graph to trends a–h.

Share prices ...

a rose (by ... to)
b fell (by ... to)
c fluctuated (between)
d plummeted (to)
e stabilised (at)
f levelled off (at)
g peaked (at)
h dipped (to)

2 Describe the graphs below to your partner. Which graph is your partner describing?

3 Listen to three speakers and answer the questions.

1 Which graph shows the annual trend in public spending?

2 Which chart illustrates the staff absentee rate?

3 Which graph compares China's trade growth with global trade growth?

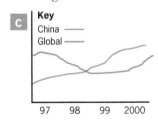

4 Listen to someone from a travel company talking about sales of different holidays. Match each holiday destination (1–5) with the correct line on the graph (a–e).

Holiday destinations

1 US/Canada
2 Europe
3 South America
4 Pacific Rim
5 India

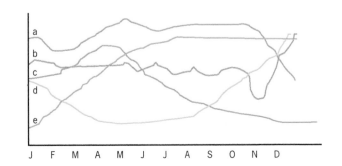

Academic Writing Task 1: Trends and verb tenses

1 Read the description of students' spending on books below, and underline the verbs.

Draw a graph to illustrate the paragraph.

> The amount of money students spend on books has risen dramatically over the past four years. Last year each student at our college spent an average of £100, whereas five years ago, they only spent £40 on average. Over the next year, it is expected that the average personal spending on books will rise to at least £120 per year.

GRAMMAR

Tenses

When describing trends in the IELTS test it is best to use:

the **simple past** to talk about 'finished' time, e.g. *yesterday, in 1997, last year*

the **present perfect** to talk about 'unfinished' time, e.g. *since 1997, ever, this month*

a **future tense** to talk about future time, e.g. *next year, tomorrow, over the next week*

We often use the following expressions when talking about future or predicted data, because the simple future is a little too certain:

… are/is (un)likely to   … are/is predicted to
… are/is expected to

For example: *The number of people travelling to Pacific Rim countries next year is predicted to rise.*

OR we use a verb such as *predict* and a future tense.

For example: *Tour operators predict that the number of people travelling to Pacific Rim countries will rise next year.*

2 Complete these predictions.

a Global temperatures .... in the next decade.

b Experts predict that more people .... smoking in the coming year.

c The birthrate in Italy .... next year.

d .... the number of visitors to London will decrease in the future.

3 Which tense would you use with each of the phrases below? Write PS for past simple, PP for present perfect and F for a future tense.

a in the 19th century   PS
b since 1995
c recently
d between 1990 and 1992
e last summer
f from 2005 to 2015
g for the last five years
h over the next decade
i a year ago
j in the coming year
k in 10 years' time
l over the past ten years

4 Complete the gaps in the description below by using an appropriate verb in the correct tense.

Over a barrel
Forecast increase in world oil production – million barrels/day

The graph gives past, present and future data concerning the production of the world's oil in OPEC and non-OPEC countries. The figures (a) .... that while the production of oil in Middle Eastern OPEC countries (b) .... to increase considerably, oil production elsewhere is likely (c) ....

Between 1980 and 2000, most of the world's oil (d) .... non-OPEC countries; only two million barrels per day (e) .... by OPEC countries. Since then, these figures (f) .... considerably. Between 2000 and 2010 it is (g) .... that approximately 10 million barrels per day (h) .... from Middle Eastern OPEC countries, while a further 10 million barrels will be provided by other OPEC or non-OPEC countries.

Although forecasters predict that oil production (i) .... to stabilise between 2010 and 2020, a lot more of this oil (j) .... to come from the Middle Eastern OPEC countries, and under 5 million barrels per day from other areas.

Step up to IELTS ACADEMIC WRITING *TASK 1*

Step 1

Read the mini exam-type task opposite.
- **What does the chart show?**
- **What does the vertical axis represent?**
- **What does the horizontal axis represent?**
- **What trend does it show?**
- **What tense will you write in?**

Take 15–20 minutes to describe the information in the chart in about 120 words. Follow Steps 2–6.

> The bar chart below gives information about vehicle ownership in China. Write a report for a university lecturer describing the information.

Step 2

Write a sentence that explains what the chart is about. Be careful not to copy the whole sentence from the task because the examiner will not rate copied material. Think of another way of saying 'vehicle ownership'. Also mention the period of time that the chart covers.

> ✓ **Test tip**
>
> Always check what the numbers refer to on the axes. These numbers are not total numbers of people. You will lose marks if you mis-read the chart.

Step 3

Write a sentence that describes the overall trend. End your first paragraph here.

Step 4

Start a new paragraph and illustrate the main stages in the trend. In this case, write two sentences that describe the trend between 1987 and 1991. Include some figures. Then, write one or two sentences that describe the trend between 1991 and 1999. Again, include some figures.

Step 5

Start a third paragraph and write a concluding sentence.

Step 6

Count the number of words you have written and check your work for mistakes.

Now do the IELTS Writing task below.

IELTS WRITING TASK

You should spend about 20 minutes on this task.

The chart below gives information about global sales of games software, CDs and DVD or video.

Write a report for a university lecturer describing the information.

You should write at least 150 words.

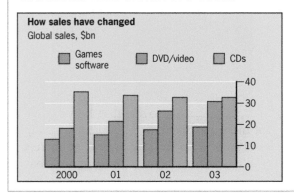

> ✓ **Test tip**
>
> 1 Don't try to explain the data. You need only describe what you see. The examiner will ignore any explanations.
>
> 2 Don't try to cover everything if you cannot do this in the word limit. Select the most significant trends and features.
>
> 3 Don't write too much. You can write more than 150 words but you will not get any extra marks for this. If you write fewer than 150 words, you may be penalised.

Useful words and phrases

approximately
about
just under/over
slightly fewer/more than
a little less/more than

IELTS Test practice

ACADEMIC WRITING Task 1

You should spend about 20 minutes on this task.

> *The chart and graph below give information about sales and share prices for Coca-Cola.*
>
> *Write a report for a university lecturer describing the information shown below.*

You should write at least 150 words.

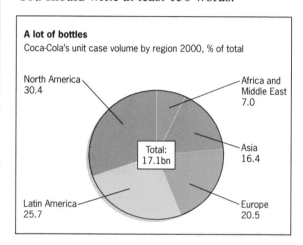

A lot of bottles
Coca-Cola's unit case volume by region 2000, % of total

North America 30.4
Africa and Middle East 7.0
Asia 16.4
Europe 20.5
Latin America 25.7
Total: 17.1bn

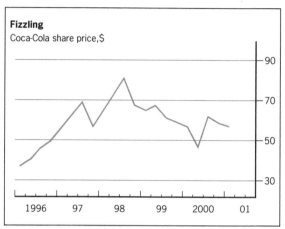

Fizzling
Coca-Cola share price, $

Remember!
- There are two tasks in the Academic Writing test and Task 2 carries more marks. So it is important to stick to the time limit suggested for Task 1.
- Task 1 may include graphs, charts, tables or other diagrams. There may be more than one diagram in the task. If this happens, the diagrams will be related in some way.
- You will lose marks if the content of your answer is inaccurate or irrelevant, or if you leave important information out.
- You must link your points well. Don't write a list or use repetitive structures.
- Marks are awarded for vocabulary and grammatical accuracy so show the examiner the range of words and structures that you know and check your answer for errors.

Approach
- Examine the diagrams carefully and decide what each one shows.
- Look for any overall trends or features first. Then decide on the best way to illustrate these. (Decide what you should include and what you need not include.) Think in terms of two or three paragraphs.
- Begin by stating clearly what the diagrams are about, but don't copy the instructions.
- Next describe the key features/trends. (You may want to divide your answer according to the material presented.)
- Support these using the most interesting or significant details. Give some figures.
- End by drawing any obvious conclusions.
- Leave time at the end to check your answer for errors in grammar, spelling and punctuation.

Ignorance is bliss

IELTS READING *PARAGRAPH HEADINGS*

In both the Academic and General Training Reading papers, you may be tested on your understanding of the main topics, themes or ideas in paragraphs. This is done through the 'Paragraph heading' task.

To get going

1 Read paragraph 1, which is taken from a college handbook. Which of the topics below best fits as a heading?
a Group tutors
b Tutorial sessions
c Student workload

2 The headings below focus on possible themes within paragraph 1. Which of these best fits?
a Looking after student welfare
b Creating the right learning situation
c Running compulsory courses

Some paragraphs are less factual than others. They offer opinions and discuss things. Paragraphs like these may have headings that are less obvious to spot.

3 Underline the main idea in paragraph 2, which comes from a teaching journal.

4 Which heading best fits? Why?
a Why students are failing courses
b Students' over-dependence on computers
c Adapt to your students' needs

When you do a paragraph heading task, the paragraphs in the reading passage will be labelled, starting with A. Your task will be to match each paragraph to the correct heading. All the other headings will be wrong and there will be some extra headings that you will not need.

Step 1

Skim through the list of headings first. Are there any words that you have not seen before? If so, can you guess their meaning? Underline any key words.

Step 2

Read paragraph A and underline the topic and main idea. Do any of the headings i–v match this? Repeat the procedure for paragraph B.

1 Students are expected to attend all tutorial sessions. These are a compulsory part of the course. The group tutor who runs these sessions is responsible for the welfare of students in his/her tutor group and the tutorials are designed to help students solve problems and discuss any matters that concern them.

2 As a teacher, it is important to become aware of your students' preferred learning styles. If you do this, you may be able to encourage students who do not respond to you as you would like them to. College students these days have often grown up with TV, video games and computers. They can interact well with machines and this may mean that they favour their use in the classroom and react badly to lectures and other more formal teaching methods.

IELTS READING TASK

Choose the correct heading i–v for each paragraph from the list of headings below.

A In order to be successful, students must be able to work alone. You should make sure that you do this regularly, in addition to attending lectures and other activities on your timetable. You may choose to work outside the college but there are also resources provided within the college to help you.

B In the Learning Resource Centre, you will find staff available to give you advice in using the facilities provided. Materials range from computer workstations and audio/video machines to specialist journals. There are areas for private study, group work and tutorials if you need extra help.

List of Headings

i Extra-curricular activities

ii Independent study

iii Who is responsible for your learning?

iv Using the college resources

v How to adapt to different teaching styles

Narration and past tenses

1 Read this description that a student has written about a former teacher and underline all the past tense verb forms.

2 Which of the verbs that you have underlined ...

  a describes a past situation that is linked to the present time?

  b describes a completed past event?

  c describes a completed past event within another past event?

3 Match the verb tenses below (1–3) with the descriptions in exercise 2 (a–c).

  1 simple past

  2 present perfect

  3 past perfect

4 Use the notes opposite to write a description of Mr Finn.

5 Complete these sentences. In each case, can you name the verb tense you used?

Example: I _have always wanted_ (always) (want) to learn Japanese but unfortunately I have never had the time. present perfect

  a It .... (take) my sister six months to learn to drive before she finally passed her driving test.

  b It .... (take) me six months to paint this picture and I'm still working on it.

  c How .... (come) to college this morning?

  d The course was a lot harder than I .... (expected) before I started my degree.

  e I .... (live) in London since I was a child and I don't think I could live anywhere else.

  f .... (apply) for an extension for your visa yet? You'd better be quick because today's the last day!

  g By the time Michael got to the library, his sister .... (already) (leave).

6 Find an example of *used to* + infinitive in the description of Mrs Huxley in exercise 1.

Write about three things that you used to do and three things that you didn't use to do.

> When I was a Form 4 student, my favourite teacher was Mrs Huxley who taught History and English. I remember she always wore very bright colours and she used to make us laugh by acting out some of the scenes from the history books. Mrs Huxley didn't bore us like other teachers because she was so entertaining. Also, you could always tell that she had done a lot of preparation before each class, which made us feel special.
> Since I became a teacher myself, I have thought about Mrs Huxley a lot. She has left the school now and I wonder if she realises that her old students haven't forgotten her!

> mr Finn
> South College Lecturer – Graphics, Fine art
> Least favourite
> Shouted a lot, lots of homework
> no groupwork or personal help
> no previous teaching experience – dull
> no interest in art for me since then

GRAMMAR

> ## *used to* + infinitive
>
> This structure is used to describe a past habit that doesn't exist now. For example:
>
> I *used to be* very hard working. (i.e. but now I am not)
> I *used to wear* glasses. (i.e. but now I don't)
>
> I *didn't use to wear* contact lenses. (i.e. but now I do)
> I *didn't use to like* learning English. (i.e. but now I do)

WRITING

Academic and General Training Writing Task 2: Forming ideas

You have to write a 250-word essay for Task 2. You will lose marks if you do not have enough ideas, so you need to develop strategies that will help you produce and organise your ideas quickly, before you start writing.

To get going

1 For each adjective, choose its opposite from the box of useful words. Which noun(s) from the box can you use with each pair of adjectives?

	adjective	opposite	noun
a	high-tech	low-tech	equipment
b	theoretical		
c	compulsory		
d	modern		
e	strict		
f	independent		
g	active		

Test tip

There is a lot of vocabulary related to the topic of education and learning. It is *all* very useful for IELTS and you should learn as much as you can.

Using your imagination and experience

2 Read the sample task opposite.
In order to write an answer to this, you need to compare formal and informal teaching methods. Exercises 3–8 will help you work towards the answer you will write in exercise 9.

> *Formal education methods, where the teacher instructs the whole class and the students work alone, are more reliable and produce better results than informal methods.*
>
> *Do you agree or disagree?*

3 Look at the two pictures below.
Use your own *experience* to say which picture is more familiar to you.

- Discuss the similarities and differences between the two pictures.
- Use your *imagination* to say which learning situation you would prefer.

4 Categorise the differences between pictures A and B by completing the table opposite. Use an adjective and support this with some evidence.

category	A	B
learning environment	Formal – teacher at front	Informal – teacher with students
classroom furniture		
student/teacher appearance		
teaching/learning style		
student behaviour		

5 Complete the short paragraph below, which compares two different learning environments.

> The learning environment in schools in my country has changed significantly. Twenty years ago, classrooms were **(a)** .... places with desks and chairs arranged in neat **(b)** .... These days, however, things are quite **(c)** .... and students often sit in **(d)** .... and work **(e)** ....

✓ **Test tip**

You can use the categories of ideas to organise your thoughts into paragraphs: one category = one paragraph.

 6 Take 15 minutes to write a short paragraph about ONE of the other categories in exercise 4.

Brainstorming opposing ideas or themes

IELTS Writing tasks often ask you to discuss opposing viewpoints or to give your opinion on issues that have two or more sides to them.

7 Imagine that you have to discuss the question at the centre of the diagram below. Read the notes that a student has made and complete the ideas/themes with an opposite.

f Active versus .... learning

e Visual versus .... materials

d Practical approach versus ....

a Discovery and research versus ....rote learning.......

b Group versus ....

c Continuous assessment versus ....

8 Choose two themes from the diagram above and develop them with further ideas/examples/reasons. An example has been done for you.

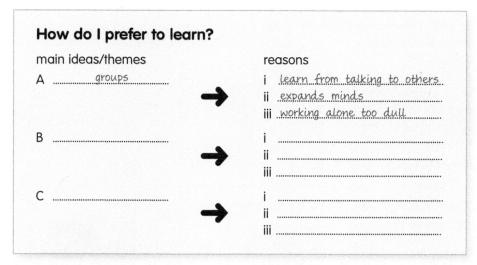

How do I prefer to learn?

main ideas/themes

A ....groups.............

B ....

C ....

reasons

i learn from talking to others
ii expands minds
iii working alone too dull

i ....
ii ....
iii ....

i ....
ii ....
iii ....

✓ **Test tip**

If you have a lot of ideas, you can't write about them all. Pick the most interesting ones and *develop* those, so that your paragraphs are coherent and have a clear structure.

 9 Read this paragraph that has been written using the notes above. Take 15 minutes to write two more paragraphs using the notes you made in exercise 8.

> An informal approach to learning often means that students learn in groups, rather than as a whole class with the teacher standing at the front. I think group learning is beneficial because you can learn from talking to other students. If you are alone all the time, you only have your own ideas to work with, whereas group learning helps you expand your mind and appreciate a range of ideas. Generally, this is more interesting than working independently.

49

Part 2: Giving a talk

In Part 2 of the Speaking test, you have to talk for one to two minutes on a topic that the examiner gives you. Before you talk, you have one minute to write notes on a piece of paper. Remember that you can lose marks for poor pronunciation in any part of the Speaking test.

Pronunciation check

To form the past tense of regular verbs in English, we add *-ed* but the *-ed* forms are not always pronounced in the same way.

1 **First, listen to the examples in the table and repeat them. Then listen to the short conversations below and decide which column the verbs belong in.**

/ɪd/	/d/	/t/
attended	played	kept

USEFUL RULES

After d and t use /ɪd/.

After vowels and voiced consonants, e.g. b, m, v, use /d/.

After unvoiced consonants, e.g. p, f, sh, use /t/.

a *I **expected** the repairs to take two days, but they **fixed** the car straight away.*

*Thank goodness! So you **arrived** in time for the wedding after all.*

b *The waiter **bumped** into the table and then **spilled** the drinks all over one of the customers. It was hilarious!*

*And I suppose everybody in the restaurant **laughed**!*

c *George **promised** to pick me up on time, but then, as usual, he **turned** up late.*

*But you **enjoyed** the evening, didn't you?*

Talking for one minute

2 **Select one of the following questions. Time yourself and see if you can talk to your partner about it for one minute.**

a Describe your old school uniform.

b Describe a special ceremony that took place at your school.

c Describe a school assignment that you once did.

d Describe a student you remember well.

e Describe the sports or social facilities at your school.

f Describe a school trip that you went on.

3 **Imagine that you have been given this topic:**

Describe a school you once attended.

You should say:
– what the school classrooms looked like
– what the teachers were like
– how the subjects were taught

and explain whether or not you feel it was a good school.

The card helps you organise your talk into three points.

- **Read the card, then take one minute to write some key words for each point.**
- **Now give your talk to your partner.**
- **Record it if you can.**

Listen to your partner's talk. Are the past tenses used and pronounced correctly?

IELTS Test practice

✓ Test tip

This is also useful practice for the Academic Reading module.

GENERAL TRAINING READING Section 2

You are advised to spend 20 minutes on Questions 1–13.

*Read this extract from a student handbook and answer **Questions 1–7.***

Instructions for International Students

Before you arrive

International students have to pay a £500 deposit to the college before they arrive. £350 of this goes towards tuition fees and the remaining £150 is used as a general deposit and refunded at the end of the course, if it is not needed to cover costs that result from breakages or other accidents. The Finance Office will provide all students with a reference number and this must be given when they contact the office about matters relating to their personal finances.

Tuition fees

All tuition fees must be paid in advance and in full for the complete year, apart from fees for Additional English which may be paid in instalments by semester. Semester fees should still be paid in advance. Students with 'special circumstances' may pay their fees as arranged prior to admission.

Refunds

1. A full refund of the tuition deposit is only possible if the student writes to the college two weeks before the course starts. Letters that arrive after this will be considered on a case-by-case basis but a deposit will only be refunded in very exceptional circumstances. If the full fees are not paid after the student arrives at college, then the deposit is not refundable under any circumstances.

2. Students may leave the college at any time during the first two weeks and expect to receive a refund of what remains of their tuition fees. In order to receive this, however, they must inform the college, in writing, of their intention to leave and this letter must reach the Finance Office within the two-week period. After this, refunds are only possible for subsequent semesters and only if there are no outstanding accommodation expenses.

3. Students may go to the Finance Office to collect cheques to cover the refund of their general deposit in the last week of the academic year. Any other book or equipment deposits may also be collected then. Students will lose their deposits if they fail to claim them within three months of leaving the college. This does not apply if students have chosen to leave their deposits in the College account because they are returning to enrol for the next academic year.

Complete the sentences below with words taken from 'Instructions for International Students'.

*Write **NO MORE THAN THREE WORDS** for each answer.*

1 The college may use up to .... of the student deposit to pay for any damage caused by the student.

2 If you want to talk about finance with someone, you will need to know your
....

3 Students do not need to pay all the course fees for ....
at the same time.

4 If you start your course and then decide to leave, you must apply for a refund within
.... of the starting date.

5 If a full fee refund is due to you, the college will first check that you do not owe anything for ....

6 Students have up to .... to collect their deposits after leaving the college.

7 All deposits held by the college may be used to help cover costs in a new
....

✓ Test tip

Remember, you must use words **from the text** here, not your own words.

IELTS Test practice

GENERAL TRAINING READING Section 2

Now read the information on page 53 and answer ***Questions 8–13*** *below.*

*The reading passage has 6 paragraphs **A–F**.*

Choose the correct heading for each paragraph, from the list of headings below.

List of Headings

i	Be prepared for different methods of assessment
ii	Mix with people from different countries
iii	Make sure your work is your own
iv	Aim to be successful on your course
v	Attend lectures regularly
vi	Don't believe everything you hear
vii	Feel free to discuss your education
viii	Don't worry about having a smart appearance
ix	Don't be afraid to speak up

8 Paragraph A

9 Paragraph B

10 Paragraph C

11 Paragraph D

12 Paragraph E

13 Paragraph F

Remember!
- There will be two texts in Section 2 and both will be related to education, training or academic study.
- You should spend about 10 minutes on each text and questions.
- The total number of words in the two texts will be about 750.
- The question formats may be any of the IELTS task types.

Approach
- Read the title of the passage. What do you expect the passage to be about?
- Do a quick read of the passage. Who do you think it has been written by and who do you think it has been written for?
- Go straight to the list of headings and read through them. Underline any key words that relate to topics or main ideas.
- Note the style of the set of headings. Are they testing facts or ideas?
- Underline the topic and main idea in the first paragraph. Then, skim the list of headings to see if there is one that matches. Repeat this procedure with each paragraph.
- If you cannot find a heading, leave that paragraph and go on to the next. You can come back to it later and you will have fewer headings to choose from then.

IELTS Test practice

STUDYING IN THE USA

A American films exaggerate things in order to excite audiences and so they present a rather odd picture of what life in the US is really like. Even if some ideas are true for certain individuals, they may not be true in general. For example, although Americans tend to be louder than people from other cultures, many of the people you meet when you study in the US will be quiet and polite.

B Americans are much more assertive than most international visitors. They use words as tools to give their views and to accomplish goals. It is expected that you will offer opinions and attempt to persuade someone to adopt your view. Take the initiative and volunteer information that will be of interest. In an interview, talk about your goals and accomplishments. Eye contact is also important. It is not a sign of disrespect, but instead an indication of openness, honesty and enthusiasm.

C You will find that teaching styles in the US are very different from those in other countries. Teaching in the US is interactive and less dependent on rote learning. Professors prefer discussion and debate to passive silence and classes are often organised in groups. Students regularly visit lecturers to ask questions about their courses and how they are doing. Your faculty will also have open office hours for students to come by and ask questions.

D Americans tend to be more informal than people from other countries. It is common for Americans to wear casual clothing to school and to greet professors by first name. Nevertheless, good manners and politeness are always appropriate. If you are courteous and polite, and dress a little more formally than your American friends, it will only reflect well on you. However, as in most countries, it would be inappropriate to wear a T-shirt and jeans to an interview.

E Unless the professor has indicated that collaboration is expected, you should produce your written work by yourself. Collaborating with fellow students on individual assignments is considered cheating. Studying with others is fine, but assignments should be completed alone. Likewise, using someone else's ideas or quoting a text without properly acknowledging the source is plagiarism. Cheating and plagiarism are grounds for failing or even expulsion.

F Your grade in most classes will be based on your scores on tests, quizzes, and assignments. If the class has a recitation or discussion section, active participation can improve your grade. The better the professor and teaching assistants know you and your work, the better they will be able to judge your progress. Good luck in your first semester!

Fit as a fiddle

Listening for specific information

Many questions in IELTS test your understanding of details or specific information so learning how to extract details from a speech or dialogue is an important listening skill.

 1 Ask and answer these questions.
  ▶ What are the best ways to keep healthy?
  ▶ What is meant by the saying 'An apple a day keeps the doctor away'?

2 Match the words in the box to the correct parts of the body in the picture.

ankle	back
elbow	knee
ribs	neck
shoulder	throat
toe	wrist

3 Why are these parts of the body important? Can you say where they are and what their main function is?
  a heart   c stomach
  b lungs   d brain

4 Listen to six conversations, all of them related to accidents, and match the conversations to the pictures. There are some extra pictures that you will not need.

1 ....   4 ....
2 ....   5 ....
3 ....   6 ....

5 Listen again and make a list of all the parts of the body the speakers mentioned.

What words did the speakers use to describe how they felt or to describe the pain? Complete the table.

conversation	parts of the body	describing discomfort or pain
1	toe	Feels like a bad burn – it's agony
2		
3		
4		
5		
6		

Step up to IELTS SPEAKING *PART 2*

In Part 2 of the Speaking test, you have to give a short talk lasting 1–2 minutes. The examiner will explain what you have to talk about and then give you a minute to read a card.

To get going

Look at the conversation below in which someone is telling a friend about an accident he had.

> I tripped on the steps outside the college yesterday, and twisted my ankle ...

> Oh how awful! I think those steps are quite dangerous. Did you hurt yourself?

FOLLOW-UP QUESTIONS
What did you do then?
How did you feel?
Did you go to the doctor?
Did you have to go to hospital?
How long did it take to get better?
How long did it take to heal?
Does it still hurt?

Have you ever hurt yourself? Ask and answer these questions. Then use the follow-up questions to find out more details.

> Have you ever hurt yourself?

> How did you do it?

> When did it happen?

> Did it hurt?

Step 1

Take 1 minute to read the card below. Then turn it over and see if you can remember the things you have to talk about.

> Describe a minor accident that you had in the past.
> You should say:
> – how the accident happened
> – what you did about it
> – how long you took to recover
> and explain how you felt about the accident.

✔ *Test tip*

You must stick to the topic otherwise you will lose marks.

Step 2

Now take 5 minutes to prepare your talk by completing the notes opposite.

Step 3

Give your talk to your partner. Get your partner to time how long it takes. Try to stick to the 2 minutes allowed. If you go over 2 minutes, your partner should stop you.

Accident: ....
How it happened: ....
....
....
What I did: ....
....
How long I took to recover: ....
How I felt: ....

✔ *Test tip*

You only have *one* minute to prepare in the real test. However, it is important to spend extra time in the classroom practising your skill at noting down useful information. This should provide the *key points* for your talk.

Step 4

Listen to the recording of a model Part 2 of the Speaking test.

Will/would, can/could

LANGUAGE CHECK

Conditional 1

I'll go to the concert on Saturday, *if I have* enough money for a ticket.

will + verb …, *if* + present simple *(The speaker intends to go.)*

Conditional 2

I'd go to the concert on Saturday, *if I had* enough money for a ticket.

would + verb …, *if* + past simple *(The speaker is unlikely to go.)*

What *would you do if you won* a luxury car in a competition? *(The listener is unlikely to win.)*

I'd sell it and buy a second-hand one and keep the rest of the money.

> Whether to use *will* or *would* depends on the tense of the verb in the subordinate *if* clause.

1 **Complete the sentences below with *will* or *would*.**

Example: My grandfather ....*would*........ be very surprised if he saw us now.

a I .... definitely marry him if he asked me to.
b People .... usually give up smoking if they are told to by their doctor.
c If we had one day without rain, that .... be a nice change!
d If the neighbours don't stop playing that music, I .... go completely mad.
e If I didn't know you better, I .... say you were crazy.

The verb *can*

There is no infinitive form of the modal *can* and there are only two real tenses.
Note how the meaning changes according to the situation.

Present simple	**Past simple**
can/can't + verb	*could/couldn't* + verb

My uncle *can see* well enough to drive, but he *can't read* without his glasses.
(i.e. He is able to drive but he is not able to read.)

I bent down to pick up a box but then I *couldn't stand up* again.
(i.e. I wasn't able to stand up.)

You *can't drive* in Australia until you are 17 years old.
(i.e. You are not allowed to drive.)

NB Could is often used in polite requests, e.g. *Could* you tell me the time?
Don't confuse it with the past form.

2 **Re-write the sentences below with an appropriate form of *can* by changing the words in italics.**

Example: I *wasn't able to* go to the concert on Friday.
       I couldn't go to the concert on Friday.

a I *know how to* play chess but I'm not a very good player.
b I got to the cinema early but I *wasn't able to* get seats.
c Men *are not allowed to* go to the Opera if they're not wearing a collar and tie.
d *Aren't you able to* come this evening? What a pity!
e I *didn't know how to* speak much English before I started this course.
f You *aren't allowed to* get a credit card until you've got a full-time job. It's so unfair!
g Because of the bad weather conditions, I *was unable to* see out of the car window.

Academic Writing Task 1: *Using noun phrases*

Noun phrases are often useful in Task 1 in order to provide information about the subject of the graph or chart. It is important that this information is clear and complete.

GRAMMAR

Noun phrases

Look at this noun phrase which has four pieces of information in it: number + overweight + people + the USA. It tells us what the graph is about.

The number of overweight people in the USA

Here is a description of the overall trend on the graph:

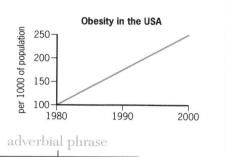

Obesity in the USA

per 1000 of population

| noun phrase | verb | adverbial phrase |

The number of overweight people in the USA + has increased + over the past twenty years.

1 **Underline the noun phrase in these sentences.**

a Statistics show that the ageing population in Europe is growing steadily.
b According to the data, children under the age of ten enjoy reading more than adults.
c The number of births per 1000 of the population is falling in some countries.
d In recent years, there has been an increase in the spread of malaria in Africa.

✓ **Test tip**

Noun phrases are often quite long!

2 **Describe the overall trend in these graphs starting with a noun phrase of at least five words. Use the word in brackets to help you decide on the tense you will use.**

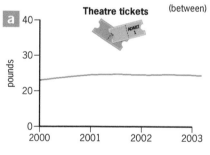

a **Theatre tickets** (between)
pounds

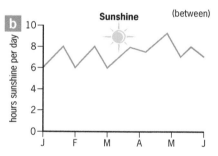

b **Sunshine** (between)
hours sunshine per day

c **Pollution from cars** (over)
metric tonnes

d **Female managers** (since)
percentage

Useful words

VERBS
rise   increase   improve
go up (by/to)   reach   fall
decrease   decline   drop
fluctuate   go down (by/to)
dip   plummet*

*this verb is so strong that it is not used with an adverb

ADVERBS/ADJECTIVES
slight(ly)   moderate(ly)
sharp(ly)   steep(ly)
dramatical(ly)
considerable(-ably)
significant(ly)

PHRASES
remain stable   level off
reach a peak/plateau

3 **Another way of describing a trend is to use the noun form of the verb within the noun phrase, e.g.** *There has been **an increase in the number of overweight people*** *in recent years.*

Re-write your sentences from exercise 2 in this way, using *There* **as the first word. Remember that the tense you use will depend on the adverb / time phrase. (See page 43.)**

WRITING

IELTS LISTENING *SECTION 2*

Section 2 is a talk by one speaker on a general topic. Most talks are divided into two parts and the questions will follow the order of information in each part. Before each part begins, you will be given some time to read through the questions.

To get going

1 **It is useful to consider what you know about the topic during the preparation time. This may help you answer some of the questions.**

> ▶ What is the Red Cross?
> ▶ What does it do?
> ▶ Where are its headquarters located?

2 **Be prepared to hear words related to the topic.**

Do you know the meaning of the words in the box? Use a good dictionary if you are uncertain. Make sure you know how they are pronounced.

Useful words

emergency   first aid   injury wounded   symbol   emblem   victim conscious   unconscious   recover preserve   protect   prevent

Step 1

Read questions 1–6. For each question, note what type of answer you need to listen for. Use the words in the question to help you. For example, for question 1 you need to listen for the name of a city or country.

Step 2

Listen to the first part of the talk and answer questions 1–6.

Step 3

Discuss what you think are the main aims of First Aid. Look at questions 7 and 8.

Step 4

Look at the bar chart and questions 9 and 10. Decide what type of information is missing. Then listen to the second part of the talk and answer questions 7–10.

IELTS LISTENING Section 2

Complete the notes. Write **NO MORE THAN THREE WORDS** *for each answer.*

Jean Henri Dunant:

– was a citizen of **1** ....

– 1859 – Italy – helped wounded soldiers – provided food and **2** ....

– 1864 – organised a conference which was the First **3** ....

Red cross chosen as emblem to symbolise their activities.

– Red Cross operates in areas of famine and **4** ....

– Misuse of the emblem is **5** ....

– In Australia the colours used to indicate First Aid are **6** .... and ....

The aims of First Aid are to:

– **7** ....

– **8** .... the victim

– prevent things from worsening

– promote recovery

Complete the chart below. Write **NO MORE THAN THREE WORDS** *for each answer.*

Accidental injuries in Australia in 1992

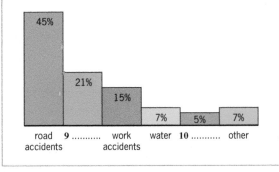

45%					
21%					
	15%				
		7%	5%	7%	
road accidents	**9**	work accidents	water	**10**	other

✔ *Test tip*

Remember that in the real test you will only hear the recording once.

IELTS Test practice

ACADEMIC READING Section 2

Questions 1–6

The reading passage has seven paragraphs A–G.

Choose the correct heading for each paragraph from the list of headings below.

List of Headings
i   Better area distribution of medicines
ii   Time for a change
iii   Research uncovers useful information
iv   A checklist of procedures introduced
v   Tackling the problem through local enquiry
vi   Excellent outcome gives hope to others
vii   Tanzania gripped by disease
viii   Immunisation programmes lack effect
ix   Aid package comes with conditions
x   The vicious cycle of poverty and illness

Test tip

There are always at least three more headings in this exercise than you need. This actually helps you because it allows you to get one answer wrong without affecting all your other answers.

Example	Answer
Paragraph **A**	x

1 Paragraph **B**
2 Paragraph **C**
3 Paragraph **D**
4 Paragraph **E**
5 Paragraph **F**
6 Paragraph **G**

Test tip

Remember what you have learnt in Units 4 and 7 about paragraphs and main ideas. These skills will help you answer paragraph heading tasks. Unit 11 also contains some follow-up work on this.

For 80 cents more
Even a tiny health budget, if spent well, can make a difference

A Delivering medicine to the world's poorest people is a challenge. Hot, poor places such as Tanzania have many microbes but microscopic health budgets. Dangerous myths deter many sick rural folk from seeking medical help. Even if they do seek help, it is often unavailable, for they do not have the money to pay for it, and their government rarely has the money to give it to them for free. Because they cannot afford adequate health care, poor people are sick a lot of the time. And because they are sick a lot of the time, they find it hard to put in the long hours of productive labour that might make them less poor.

B All hope is not lost, however. A recent experiment in Tanzania has shown that a small health budget can go a long way, provided that the money is spent with care. With the help of a Canadian charity called the International Development Research Center (IDRC), the Tanzanian health ministry set up a health project in two rural districts, to the west of the capital Dar es Salaam, with a combined population of about 700,000. Five years ago, annual health spending in Tanzania was about $8 a head. This figure included an estimate for the annual cost of trained staff and buildings devoted to health care. The IDRC added $2 a head to the pot, on condition that it was spent rationally. By this, the donors meant that the amount of money spent on fighting a particular disease should reflect the burden that disease imposed on the local population.

C This may sound obvious; however, in this region, no one had a clue which diseases caused the most trouble, so the first task was to find out. Researchers were sent out on bicycles to carry out a door-to-door survey, asking representative households whether anyone had been ill or died recently, and if so with what symptoms. These raw numbers were then crunched to produce a 'burden of disease' profile for the two districts. In other words, researchers sought to measure how many years of life were being lost to each disease, including the damage done to families when breadwinners[1] die.

D They then compared their results with the amount spent by the local health authorities on each disease and found that it bore no relation whatsoever to the harm which the disease inflicted on local people. Some diseases were horribly neglected, such as malaria, which accounted for 30% of the years of life lost but only 5% of the health budget. A cluster of childhood problems, including pneumonia, diarrhoea, malnutrition and measles, constituted 28% of the disease burden, but received only 13% of the budget. Other conditions, meanwhile, attracted more than their fair share of cash. Tuberculosis, which accounted for less than 4% of years of life lost, received 22% of the budget. Vaccinations also appeared to be over-emphasised though the low incidence of vaccine-preventable disease was probably a result of successful vaccination.

E This tiny infusion of cash from the Canadians, in the form of an extra $2 a head, was enough to allow the district health authorities to make their spending reflect the disease burden and smoothed the transition to a more effective approach to health care. Health workers, mostly nurses or paramedics rather than doctors, were given a set of rules on how to treat common symptoms. For example, if a child arrives coughing, and with a running nose and a hot brow, the nurse is instructed to work through the checklist of other symptoms to determine whether it is merely a cold or something worse. If the child is breathing more than 50 times a minute, for example, he is assumed to have pneumonia, given an antibiotic and checked again after two days. In most cases, the cheapest treatments are offered first. Children with diarrhoea are given oral re-hydration salts, which cost a few cents. If the salts fail to work, the child is referred to a clinic for treatment.

F Drugs are ordered according to what is needed; previously, the government had sent out the same package of pills to all areas. Non-malarial mountain villages received as many malaria drugs as mosquito-infected lowland ones, and areas where no one had ever suffered from asthma received asthma pills. In addition to the improved drug allocation, people are now encouraged to use bednets impregnated with insecticide as protection from mosquitoes and even the Masai, a fiercely conservative tribe of nomadic cattle-herders, have started draping themselves in insecticide-soaked bednets.

[1] The people in the household who earn the money

G The results of all this were stunning. Infant mortality fell by 28% between 1999 and 2000 and the proportion of children dying before their fifth birthday dropped by 14%. In nearby districts and in Tanzania as a whole, there is no evidence of a similar improvement over the same period, and anecdotal evidence suggests that better health has made the districts less poor. Could this success be repeated elsewhere?

The government is keen that the lessons learned be applied in other parts of the country. So keen, in fact, that it is pushing the organisers to move faster than they would prefer. Other countries could also copy the Tanzanian model and donors should pay heed that, while more money is certainly needed to tackle poor countries' health problems, how it is spent is more important than how much is spent.

Questions 7–11

Complete the summary below with words taken from the reading passage. Use **NO MORE THAN THREE WORDS AND/OR A NUMBER** *for each answer.*

SUMMARY

Citizens of developing countries are often not wealthy enough to pay for medical treatment. In addition, **7**... may prevent people from seeing a doctor. When they do, there is limited money available for treatment. The $8 a head formerly spent in Tanzania included an allocation for trained staff as well as for **8**... . The IDRC offered to increase this by **9**... as long as the money was allocated appropriately.

Research showed that the **10**... in Tanzania had been unevenly distributed in previous years so strategies were implemented to help redress this. The project has shown that improvements in **11**... appear to have brought improved prosperity to the districts where it took place.

> ✓ **Test tip**
>
> The Step-up activity on page 25 focuses on summary completion. This summary tests your understanding of the overall content of the passage.

Questions 12–14

Answer the following questions using **NO MORE THAN THREE WORDS AND/OR A NUMBER** *from the reading passage.*

12 What term is used to compare the relative effects of different diseases on a society?

....

13 Which areas of the country suffer most from malaria?

....

14 By what percentage did childhood deaths decline during the project?

....

> ✓ **Test tip**
>
> These questions target small factual details in the text.

The driving force

Expanding your answer

In Part 1 of the Speaking test, the examiner will expect you to give reasons for your answers. In Parts 2 and 3, he or she will expect you to expand more. This means that you will need to link your ideas and talk in longer sentences.

1 How do you prefer to travel? Why?

> ## Linking words
>
> *So*, *because*, *as* and *since* can be used to link causes or reasons to their outcomes. They help us to expand on a question or topic. For example:
>
> linking word
> |
> I live in the city so I prefer a small car
> clause giving reason   result

2 Read this short speech and ...
  - ▶ draw a circle around the linking words
  - ▶ underline the result in each sentence
  - ▶ draw a wavy line (〰) under the reason.

> *I prefer travelling by bike as it's much easier. In my town ... well ... it's very difficult to park because of all the traffic and parking regulations. I hate wasting time driving around looking for a place so I usually take my bike.*

3 What is the difference in sentence order when you use *so* and when you use *because*?

4 Put a suitable linking word in each space.

> (a) .... we have five people in our family we need to have a large, four-door car (b) .... we can all get in! I'd prefer to have a sports car (c) .... I love them, but (d) .... I have so many other people to consider, I don't have much choice.

> *Because* links two **clauses**, whilst *because of* is followed by a **noun** or **noun phrase**.
>
> For example: The drive to the airport is quicker now *because* the council has built a new highway.
>   The drive to the airport is quicker now *because of* the new highway.
>
> Sometimes you can use either of these linking words to express an idea but they are not always interchangeable. If you want to stress the *action* or *process*, it is best to use *because*.
>
> (*Since* is slightly formal and is more often used in written English.)

> ✓ **Test tip**
>
> If you do not try to use a variety of linking words to join your ideas, you will lose marks.

5 Link the sentences below in *three* ways using a different linking word each time. If necessary, re-order the information. Check your punctuation when you have finished.

  a I'm a vegetarian.   I don't believe in killing animals for food.
  b I'm a little short-sighted.   Sometimes I need to wear my glasses.
  c I don't like busy cities.   I spent a lot of time in the countryside when I was a child.
  d I hired a large car in Australia.   The distances are huge and petrol is relatively cheap.
  e I've lost my umbrella.   I'll buy a new one.

Part 1 – Review

6 Ask and answer the questions about car travel. As you listen, use a table like this to note how your partner answers the questions.

Q	answer	reason	linking word
a	yes	fast and convenient	because
b			
c			

 a *Do you like travelling by car?*

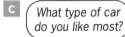 **b** *How important is image to you?*

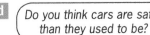 **c** *What type of car do you like most?*

d *Do you think cars are safer than they used to be?*

Academic Writing Task 1: Comparing data

Some IELTS writing tasks ask you to describe a chart or table that shows how people compare different things and how important they feel these things are in relation to each other.

Features:
sun roof
colour
air bag
stereo system
air conditioning
alarm

1 Make a table like the one opposite. Write all the features of the car above in the first column of your table. Next, in the 'personal rating' column number the features 1–6, using 6 for the most important feature and 1 for the least important when buying a car. Ignore the 'class total' and 'class rating' columns for now.

Exchange tables with a partner.

name:	Lu Liu		
features	personal rating	class total	class rating
sun roof	3	24	2
colour	4	45	4

To describe your partner's table you need to use expressions like these: *the most, the second most, the third most, the least, a little/lot more … than.* If you are not sure how to use these phrases, do this small exercise first.

2 **Look at the list of petrol prices and complete the sentences using expressions from the box above.**

Example: The most expensive day to buy petrol is ......Saturday.......

a The second most ....
b The third ....
c The .... expensive day to buy petrol is Tuesday.
d On Wednesday, petrol prices go up, but they are only
.... than on Tuesday.

Petrol prices

Mon	85c	a litre
Tues	83c	a litre
Wed	86c	a litre
Thurs	90c	a litre
Fri	95c	a litre
Sat	97c	a litre
Sun	94c	a litre

3 Now write some sentences describing your partner's rating of the features above. Select the three most important features and the least important feature.

Example:

Celia rated an airbag as the most important feature. She considered air conditioning to be the second most important feature and a sun roof, the third. She thought these features were a lot more important than an alarm or a stereo system. The least important feature for her was the colour of the car.

Useful verbs

When describing the choices or selections that people have made, the following verbs are useful:

state/say that … is/are …
feel/think/believe that … is/are …
rate + noun phrase (as)
consider/find + noun phrase (to be)
prefer … to …

4 **Add up the ratings of everyone in the class for each feature and write these totals in the 'class total' column of your table. Re-number them 1–6, using 1 for the lowest total (i.e. the least important feature) and 6 for the highest total (most important) and put these numbers in the 'class rating' column. (See the example in exercise 1.)**

5 **Draw a bar chart to show how your own ratings compare with those of the class. Start with the feature that you considered least important, as illustrated here.**

Example:

Key
personal rating   class rating

---

also, as well, too, however, similarly

Also can be used to introduce an idea that supports, or adds additional information to your main point.
It can go before the verb: *He also likes …* or between an auxiliary verb and a participle: *He has also been …, He is also coming …*
If it comes at the beginning of the sentence, put a comma after it.
As well / too come at the end of the clause or sentence.
However can be used to introduce a contrasting or surprising idea but it cannot be used to join two clauses like the word *but*. If it comes at the beginning of the sentence, put a comma after it. If, however, it comes in the middle of a sentence, put commas round it.
Similarly is used at the start of a sentence to link two similar facts or ideas.

---

6 **How does your rating compare with the rest of the class? Discuss these questions with a partner.**

▶ Is anything generally true (e.g. the personal rating always agrees with the class rating except for …)?

▶ What are the most significant features of your chart?
  – Are there any big differences? → Use a contrast word/expression e.g. *but, although, however, on the other hand, whereas.*
  – Are there any clear similarities? → Combine ideas using *similarly, also, as well* or *too.*

▶ Can you draw any conclusions from the data? Do they show anything interesting or surprising?

7 **Before you describe your bar chart, read the description of the sample chart and fill the spaces with a linking word or phrase.**

> The bar chart compares my personal ratings of six car features with the ratings of the whole class.
> Generally, the chart shows quite a lot of differences in our ratings, a) ...., we do agree on two of the features. I rated colour as the third most important feature and the class did too.
> b) .... we all considered an airbag to be the second most important feature. c) ...., I felt that a stereo system was the most important feature, d) ....the class rated this as least important. e) ...., the least important feature for me was air conditioning, which the class considered a lot more important.
> f) ...., the class rated security and safety above comfort, g) .... surprisingly, we all gave colour quite a lot of significance.

8 **Take 20 minutes to describe your bar chart. Remember to use paragraphs and …**
  ▶ say what the chart shows
  ▶ summarise any overall trends
  ▶ highlight the main features
  ▶ draw any relevant conclusions.

9 **Sometimes ratings are turned into percentages, as in the bar chart opposite. In this case, the people who were interviewed ticked the skills that they found most difficult.**

Take 20 minutes to describe this chart.

✔ *Test tip*

IELTS charts often have an 'other' category. In this case, it means 'other *skills*' besides the ones listed. Don't ignore this category. Remember that 'other' is an adjective. Decide what the noun is and then describe the statistic.

What drivers rate most difficult

% 50
   40
   30
   20
   10
   0
   reversing parking keeping to speed limit hill starts other

Useful words

Generally
Interestingly
Surprisingly
Predictably

Recognising the structure of a passage

Some IELTS passages have a clear structure and if you take note of this, it may help you to find the answers to questions.

First reading

Take 30 seconds to skim the passage and decide what it's about.

a The passage divides neatly into two halves. Where would you draw the line between these?

b Write a sentence explaining what the two halves are about.

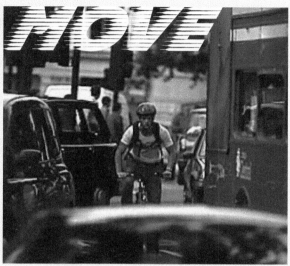

Getting from A to B as quickly and easily as possible is one of the pre-requisites of modern life. But how can this be reconciled with our need to give the planet a rest?

Clunk, click, vroom – and away we go. Every day millions of us climb into our cars and set off on journeys to work, the shops or just to enjoy ourselves. And once inside our cars, few of us are inclined to spare a thought for the environmental impacts of driving. Advertising consistently portrays cars as symbols of personal status and freedom and sources of comfort and convenience.

But behind the shiny commercials, the costs of our car-borne lifestyles are becoming increasingly serious. The lengthening traffic jams, demands for new roads, increasing air pollution and threat of climate change are all issues we must tackle sooner rather than later.

Emissions from transport are the fastest-growing source of greenhouse-gas pollution – mainly in the form of CO_2 arising from the combustion of petrol and diesel. About a fifth of UK greenhouse gases now comes from road transport, with the proportion set to rise as road traffic does (currently growing by about one per cent a year). The economic impact of congestion is costing us billions, while transport pollution is estimated to lead annually to the premature death of more than 20,000 people. Controversial new road schemes, though fewer in number than during the 1990s, are still an issue, with some threatening nationally important wildlife areas.

But what about the solutions? The top priority in the short term is to avoid as much non-essential car use as we can. At the same time, we need to introduce new technologies that will reduce the impact of car use. And we need to introduce them soon – not least to assist those countries where road traffic is rapidly increasing. For example, if China was to have one or two cars in most households and was to consume fuel at the rate of US drivers, then there would be an additional demand for oil of some 80 million barrels a day – more than the present total global output. With these kinds of projections in mind, it is clear that new vehicle technology is vital.

Vehicle designers are well aware that they need to come up with cars that have a low environmental impact. This won't solve congestion or lessen the pressure traffic creates for new roads, but new transport technologies could make car use sustainable and non-polluting and become important new industries. And as in the case of electricity generation, it is not a question of *if* we will make such a transition, it is more a question of *how*.

The best solution is not to drive at all. Walking and cycling can be perfectly viable alternatives in many situations. Public transport is another option, and again results in clearer roads and cleaner air. But for those journeys where a car is indispensable, what are the options?

IELTS READING TRUE/FALSE/NOT GIVEN

You may be asked to say whether a statement agrees with the information in the passage, whether it contradicts the information (i.e. it is the opposite) or whether the writer says nothing about this.

✔ **Test tip**

You may *think* that a question is true but you must find evidence in the passage. If you cannot, the answer is likely to be 'NOT GIVEN'.

Step 1

Look at question 1 in the IELTS Reading task opposite and decide whether you *think* it will be true from your first reading of the passage on page 65. Then ask yourself:

a What are the key words in the statement?

b Can you find something in the first paragraph that has the same meaning as the statement in question 1?

Step 2

Go on to question 2 and scan the passage for the key words, *advertisers* and *other products*, or something similar.

a What does the passage say about 'advertisers'? Express this idea in your own words.

b Does the statement in question 2 mean the same, the opposite, or neither? What is missing?

Step 3

a What are the key words in question 3?

b Is the question likely to be true? Find the answer.

c Write True, False or Not Given, depending on your answer.

Step 4

Take 5 minutes to do questions 4–8.

Step 5

Take 5 minutes to complete the summary, questions 9–13.

IELTS READING TASK

Questions 1–8

Do the following statements agree with the information in the reading passage?

Write

TRUE   *if the statement agrees with the information*
FALSE   *if the statement contradicts the information*
NOT GIVEN *if there is no information on this*

1 People use cars for a variety of purposes.

2 Advertisers prefer promoting cars to other products.

3 People have stopped asking for new roads.

4 Cars produce fifty per cent of the UK's greenhouse gases.

5 More people are learning to drive every year.

6 There were more controversial plans to build new roads in the 1990s than now.

7 The Chinese use as much petrol as the Americans.

8 At present the world uses 80 million barrels of oil a day.

Questions 9–13

Complete the summary using words from the box.

There is now an **9** .... among car designers of the need to reduce the **10** .... problems caused by cars. The technologies required to do this could lead to the creation of new **11** ....

However, one solution is to use **12** .... , as this would cut down on traffic and also result in cleaner **13** ....

buses	agreement	congestion	lives
damage	bicycles	pollution	awareness
solution	industries	roads	air
arrangement	transport	lifestyles	

IELTS Test practice

LISTENING Section 2

Questions 1–10

Questions 1–5

Complete the notes using **NO MORE THAN THREE WORDS**.

'Firsts' in the History of the Car

- Word 'automobile' first used by Italian painter in 14th century

- 'Car' comes from a Latin word that means **1** ....
  or ....

- 1839 – first electric-powered road vehicle built in
  2 ....

- Late 1800s – electric **3** .... first used in London

- First cars called **4** ....
  ....

- Early 1900s – first cars sold in
  5 .... shops

Remember!
- You will only hear the recording once, so you must answer the questions as you listen.
- Section 2 is always a monologue.
- The topic for Section 2 is always a social/general one. The situation may be formal or informal.
- Section 2 is usually divided into two parts.
- The questions here are sentence and table completion, but you may get any type of IELTS question in the Listening sections.

Approach
- Before the recording begins, read the questions carefully and try to predict the type of answer that you will need.
- If you cannot do a question, ignore it and go on to the next one. Don't waste time worrying about the answer.
- Spell all answers correctly when you write them on the answer sheet.

Questions 6–10

Complete the table using **NO MORE THAN THREE WORDS AND/OR A NUMBER**.

Biography of Henry Ford

Date	Event	Details
1863	Born	Son of Irish **6** ....
1879	Built an internal-combustion engine	Used plans from a **7** ....
1896	Built the 'Quadricycle'	Raised capital for more creations
1903	Founded the **8**	Model A car cost $850 to buy
1906	Lost money with the Model K	It was **9** .... and ....
1914	Opened the first car assembly line for the Model T	It took **10** .... to put together a car

LISTENING

Reading ahead

In all parts of the Listening test it is important to keep reading ahead as you write. If you miss an answer, just go on to the next question.

1 Ask and answer these questions.

▶ What was the last film that you saw? Did you enjoy it?
▶ Which actor do you like the most? Why?

▶ What do you know about Hollywood?
▶ What does 'the silver screen' mean?

2 Answer the questions.

a What is a biography?
b What is the difference between a biography and an autobiography?
c What sort of information do you expect to find in a biography?

3 Take 45 seconds to silently read through the questions below.

Then re-phrase each question in your own words,
e.g. Q1 = 'Where was she born?'

Listen to two students talking about the actress
Nicole Kidman and answer the questions as you listen.

✔ *Test tip*

The answers to the questions will come in the same order on the recording. You should have time to write each answer while you are listening for the next answer.

Nationality:	Australian
Place of birth:	1 .... USA
Childhood interests:	2 .... and ....
Hair colour: red	Height: 3 ....
Date of first film:	4 ....
First famous film: *Dead Calm*	Type of film: 5 ....
First film with Tom Cruise:	*Days of* 6 ....
Golden Globe Award	for 7 .... in *To Die For.*
2001:	8 .... Tom Cruise
Latest interest:	9 ....

4 Listen to the extract again and complete the responses.

a *Well, we know that she's Australian.*

She .... in Australia from the age of four, but she .... in Honolulu.

b *She was taller than Tom Cruise.*

But he .... mind. He .... in love with her and they .... in 1990.

c *Does she always star in the same type of film?*

No, ... in many different films.

For each one, name the verb tense and explain why it has been used.

Expressing and justifying views

In Part 3 of the Speaking test, the examiner will ask you to discuss some points that he or she raises. These will be thematically linked to your Part 2 topic.

1 **Look at the list of film types. Think of the films you have seen recently. Which types of film are they?**

Action	Comedy	Musical
Drama	Fantasy	Western
Horror	History	Martial arts
Romance	Cartoon	Teen movie
Science fiction	Crime	Thriller

2 **Which type of film are the people below talking about?**

a   The idea of life on Venus is so far-fetched!
b   I laughed all through the film.
c   The suspense had me on the edge of my seat.
d   I'm not very keen on love stories.
e   I don't like films where the actors suddenly start singing.
f   I loved the part where the cat played the piano and the mouse danced on the table.
g   The film ended when the sheriff shot the bad guy.
h   I couldn't look when the vampire caught his victim.

3 **Make some comparative and superlative sentences about films / actors / directors / scenes, etc. and explain to your partner why you have these opinions. Use the Sentence starters to help you.**

> **SENTENCE STARTERS**
> The best worst film I've ever seen is …
> The best scene in … is when …
> My least favourite type of film is …
> I don't like … as much as …
> This is because …

Useful words

special effects
character   part
scene   scenery

frightening
amusing
exciting
convincing

4 **Tell your partner what you think about some of the film types above, using words from the box below.**

> like/dislike   because (of)   as long as   however   at all   find   as   provided that   whereas   really   prefer   so   if   even though   too

Example:

> *I like martial arts films as long as they have a good story line. 'Crouching Tiger Hidden Dragon' was good because the plot was interesting and the characters were very believable. But some other martial arts films … well, I'm not as keen on them, as there are so many special effects.*

Test tip

You must show that you have enough vocabulary to discuss non-personal topics in the test.

GRAMMAR

▸ *as long as / provided that*

In spoken English it is common to use *as long as*, *providing* or *provided (that)* to express conditions relating to the present or future. For example:

I don't mind eating meat *as long as* it's well cooked. (*i.e. if it is well cooked*)

I'll finish this essay tomorrow *provided (that)* my computer's working. (*i.e. if my computer's working*)

Test tip

The examiner will be checking to see if you can use complex sentences. You will get credit for this, even if you make mistakes.

Dealing with longer passages

IELTS reading passages are long (about 900 words). In order to answer the questions you first need to have a good understanding of the overall content.

First reading

1 Take 3 minutes to do a quick read of the passage below and note down three interesting facts about Indian cinema.

2 **Decide whether the passage is**
   a a descriptive text   b a chronological account   c an analysis of research

Second reading

3 Take 5 minutes to read the passage and underline the main idea in each paragraph.

The appeal and success of Bollywood movies has become a worldwide phenomenon

Indian films are the most widely seen movies in the world. And the audiences are not found solely within India itself, where 12 million people are said to go to the cinema every day. They are also found in Russia, China, the Middle East, South East Asia, Britain and Africa. People from very different cultural and social worlds have a great love for Indian popular cinema, and many have been fans of Hindi films for over fifty years.

India releases a staggering number of films. Recent sources estimate that around 800 films a year are made in different cities including Madras, Bangalore, Calcutta and Bombay. However, of this astonishing number, the films made in Bombay, in both the Hindi and Urdu languages, have the widest distribution within India and internationally. The two sister languages are spoken in six northern states and understood by over 500 million people. For this reason, they were chosen to become the languages of Indian popular cinema when sound came to the Indian silver screen in 1931.

In the early 1990s, there was an incredible growth of cable, satellite and television channels in Asia. Many of these were beamed in from Hong Kong. At first, Indian film producers feared that the popularity of Hindi films would decrease because of the new multi-channel competition. However, they soon realised that television gave their films an even greater reach, not only in India but throughout Asia. Half-hour programmes showing film songs, star interviews and the movies themselves have become a major part of television programming. As a result, Hindi cinema has never enjoyed as much influence as it has today; it is at the heart of popular culture in Indian big cities, influencing music, fashion and the world of entertainment.

Recently, the Hindi film industry has become universally known as 'Bollywood' – some people claim a journalist from the popular Indian film magazine *Cineblitz* first introduced the term in the 1980s. The Bollywood name has divided critics, filmmakers and stars, many of whom refuse to use it. They believe it sets up Hindi cinema against Hollywood movies in an overly simplified way. But despite such valid protests, the term has become common currency in both India and elsewhere. Most people find it a useful way of identifying Bombay productions, perhaps seeing Bollywood movies as a product of large-scale entertainment much in the same way as Hollywood films are regarded.

Any Bollywood film juggles several genres and themes at the same time. However, audiences are used to the sometimes extreme shifts in tone and mood. A violent action scene can be followed by a dialogue in which a mother tells her son never to be dishonest, and this exchange can then be followed by a comic scene led by one of the film's secondary characters. It is precisely this mix of genres that makes the Bollywood film unique. The multi-genre film was known in the 1970s and 80s as the 'masala' film – the term comes from the idea that, like curry cooked with different spices, or masala, the Hindi film offers a variety of flavours.

The average Hindi film does not pretend to offer a unique storyline. If the audience is looking for originality, they know it is principally to be found in the music. The song and dance sequences are the most important moments – even more so today. Film music is of such primary importance in today's Bollywood that it more or less determines the box-office fate of most movies. Leading choreographer Farah Khan believes that, 'What is saving Indian cinema from being engulfed by Hollywood is our song and dance routines, because they just can't imitate that.'

Audiences know that the films offer more than just happy endings. The stories are full of hope, showing that good inevitably triumphs: the poor man defeats the rich man; the rich heroine is able to marry below her class and continue to enjoy a good lifestyle; people live modern westernised lives and still respect traditional Indian values; the hero always beats the villain and the dark side of life is banished forever. The most famous of all Indian film stars, Amitabh Bachchan, sums it all up: 'Hindi films provide poetic justice in just three hours – a feat that none of us can achieve in a lifetime.'

IELTS READING PICKING FROM A LIST

Some IELTS questions ask you to select correct answers from a list. This is a bit like an extended multiple-choice question.

Step 1

In questions 1–3 take statements A–F one at a time. For A, quickly scan the text to find references to television. Then read that section more closely to see whether statement A is the same as what is said in the passage or not.

> Discourse marker 'At first' shows their initial fears didn't last

> In the early 1990s, there was an incredible growth of cable, satellite and television channels in Asia. Many of these were beamed in from Hong Kong. <u>At first</u>, Indian film producers feared that the popularity of Hindi films would decrease because of the new multi-channel competition. <u>However,</u> they soon realised that television gave their films <u>an even greater reach</u>, not only in India but throughout Asia.

> Unusual use of 'reach' as a noun. Guess the meaning. This and 'even greater' provide the key.

> Marker that introduces the real effect of TV programmes.

Step 2

Do the same for statement B and then go on to the next statement.

 Test tip

American words and spellings are acceptable in IELTS. The American words *movie*, which means 'film' or *movies* which means 'cinema' are commonly used.

Step 3

At the end, check that you have chosen the correct number of statements. If you have too many or not enough you should go back and re-check your answers.

Step 4

Take 8 minutes to answer questions 4–9.

Step 5

Some IELTS passages end with a global multiple-choice question that tests your understanding of the overall content or the purpose of the passage.

Take 2 minutes to answer question 10.

IELTS READING TASK

Questions 1–3

Choose **THREE** letters A–F.

According to the passage, which **THREE** of the following statements are true of Bollywood movies?

A They have lost audiences since the growth of TV films.
B Some Indian film stars dislike the name Bollywood.
C The films have one clear main idea.
D The plot is often well known.
E Music is a secondary feature in the films.
F Justice is an important element of the film story.

Questions 4–9

Do the following statements agree with the information in the reading passage?

Write
TRUE   *if the statement agrees with the information*
FALSE   *if the statement contradicts the information*
NOT GIVEN *if there is no information on this*

4 More people go to the cinema in India than in China.
5 Bollywood films have only recently become popular internationally.
6 Bollywood films are produced in six different languages.
7 Talking movies were first introduced in India in the 1930s.
8 Bollywood films have a direct effect on Indian lifestyles.
9 The popularity of Indian films increased the popularity of Indian food.

Question 10

10 What is the purpose of the passage?
   A to review the latest Bollywood films
   B to compare Hollywood and Bollywood films
   C to explain what Bollywood films are
   D to predict the future of Bollywood films

 Test tip

For an answer to be FALSE, the statement must mean the opposite of what is said in the passage.

SPEAKING

Part 2 review

In Part 2 of the Speaking test, you have to give a short talk lasting 1–2 minutes. The examiner will explain what you have to talk about and then give you a minute to read a card.

1 **Take 1 minute to read the card below. Then turn it over and see if you can remember the things you have to talk about.**

> Describe a film that you particularly like.
>
> You should say:
>
> ◆ what type of film it is and what it is about
> ◆ what happens in the film
> ◆ what sort of people you think would enjoy the film
>
> and explain why you particularly like this film.

Test tip

You must keep to the topic, otherwise you will lose marks.

2 **Take 5 minutes to prepare your talk by making some notes similar to the notes below.**

Name of film: _The Matrix_

Type of film: _Science fiction / futuristic_

Storyline: _Robots have made humans into slaves to run their society / fake world_

Who would like it: _young people / computer fans_

My reasons for liking it: _good special effects_
good plot – twist at the end

3 **Give your talk to a partner and also record it, if possible. Begin your talk:**

'The film I have chosen is …'

As you are speaking, practise looking at your notes to remind you of each main point and remember to look directly at your partner.

As you listen to your partner's talk, time them and see if they have covered everything on this checklist:

Did your partner ...	Yes/No
... look at you?	
... talk for 1–2 minutes?	
... keep to the topic?	
... cover all the points on the card?	
... talk clearly?	
... talk at a steady speed?	
... use intonation and word stress?	
... use appropriate vocabulary for the topic?	

IELTS Test practice

GENERAL TRAINING WRITING Task 2

(This task is also suitable practice for the Academic Module. See page 91.)

You should spend about 40 minutes on this task.

Write about the following topic.

> *Some people warn that the era of the silver screen is coming to an end and that people will eventually lose interest in going to the cinema.*

> *Do you agree or disagree with this view? Give reasons for your answer and include any relevant examples from your experience.*

You should write at least 250 words.

Remember!

- If you are asked to agree or disagree it does not matter whether you argue for or against a topic, as long as your arguments are clear.
- The examiner should be able to identify your main ideas and your supporting points.
- You need to include some examples to illustrate your points.
- It often helps to discuss the topic in relation to your own culture or society.
- A short introduction and conclusion should be included.
- You will lose marks if you write fewer than 250 words.
- You will lose marks if your answer is irrelevant to the topic.
- Your handwriting should be clear.

Approach

- Take five minutes to plan your essay.
- Write in paragraphs and include a main point in each paragraph.
- Use a range of vocabulary and try to include phrases as well as words.
- Use a range of formal structures suitable for essay writing.
- Try to link your ideas well using different words and phrases.
- Leave time at the end to check your answer for errors in grammar, spelling and punctuation.

READING

Identifying main and supporting ideas

The best overall preparation for IELTS is to read as widely as possible, so that you develop your vocabulary and your ideas about popular topics. This will help you in ALL parts of the test. When you read a passage for IELTS, it is important to note these things: the topic, the main idea and the development of the main idea. IELTS Reading questions often test your understanding of main ideas and supporting points.

1 **Ask your partner which of the following things they enjoy reading. Tick the choices they make. Ask them why they enjoy these. Then ask them what they most like to read.**

fiction / non fiction	plays	newspapers
textbooks	poetry	picture books
guidebooks	journals	cartoons/comics
manuals	magazines	internet material

2 **Look at the adjectives in the box. Which adjectives could you use with each type of reading material above?**

Example: *fiction* – *light, imaginative, challenging, dull, relaxing, well/badly written*

✔ Test tip

Adjectives tell people more about your feelings and opinions. They help you describe these in the Writing and the Speaking parts of the test and they help you understand other people's opinions in the Reading and Listening parts of the test. Build up a list of useful adjectives.

Useful adjectives

interesting	challenging
light	dull
straightforward	relaxing
realistic	informative
illustrated	well/badly written
imaginative	amusing

3 **Take 10 seconds to skim paragraph A opposite and say what the *topic* is.**

4 **Read the paragraph again and underline the *main idea*.**

5 **What do you notice about where the main idea comes in the paragraph?**

6 **The main idea is developed through examples. List the examples:**

a ....

b ....

c ....

Do you agree with the writer's view?

A The wonder of being on holiday is that you can read the things that you don't have to read for work or study. A lawyer, for instance, may have 16 boxes of files to read before lunch on the collapse of a business. For doctors, it's endless patients' notes and medical journals. Literary journalists are surrounded by towers of books to review, or press cuttings on the next author to interview. This is not reading as it once was; it is information extraction. All year people read in a utilitarian fashion, thinking how best to use the words in front of them. On holiday, while the body begins to rest and recover, the mind can rediscover reading as it ought to be: as mental freedom.

7 Take 1 minute to skim paragraph B and note down the topic, main idea and development.

B Logophilia is the name given to the love of words. 'Logo' means word and 'phil' comes from the Greek language and means love. Many people consider it an illness and adults who suffer from it are very easy to recognise. They <u>regularly ask</u> you what books you are reading; they <u>lean over</u> someone on a train in order to discover what they are reading; they <u>eagerly take up</u> membership of every library in the area and they <u>linger</u> in bookshops far longer than the average person. Is anyone you know a logophile?

8 In the development of the main idea, the same grammatical structure is repeated in lines 5, 6, 7 and 9. This is one way of including the supporting points in a paragraph. What effect do you think it has?

Why is the present simple tense used?

9 Re-write paragraph A using the same technique of repeating grammatical structures.

Does this improve the paragraph?

10 Take 20 seconds to underline the five words which express the main idea in paragraph C below.

C What is the connection between bestselling fiction and a bestselling drink? In a recent survey on the subject of things which can help you recover from flu, Lucozade (a well-known British health drink) and popular fiction came third and fourth. First and second places were taken by watching a morning TV show and tender loving care from a loved one. The belief that books are good for you has existed for some time. Perhaps the doctor should say, 'Here's a prescription for a light romantic novel. Take it to your local library.'

What do you notice about the listing technique in this paragraph?
What is the function of the last two sentences?

11 Take 2 minutes to answer the following multiple-choice questions. Choose the correct letter A, B, C or D.

1 In paragraph A, the writer's main point is that
 A different people read different things.
 B lawyers have little time to read for pleasure.
 C serious readers prefer informative reading material.
 D holidays provide an opportunity for relaxed reading.

2 According to paragraph B, logophiles are easy to spot because they
 A look tired and ill.
 B try to read anything available.
 C prefer bookshops to other stores.
 D are too busy to see their friends.

3 In paragraph C, why does the writer compare reading with Lucozade?
 A because they both help people get better
 B because he prefers TV to both of them
 C to encourage people to read more
 D to make libraries more popular

Test tip

There are two types of four-option multiple-choice questions. In one you have to answer a question (e.g. Q3) and in the other you have to complete a sentence (e.g. Qs 1 and 2).

NB You only need to write the letter A, B, C or D on your answer sheet.

READING

Adverbs

Adverbs tell us more about verbs (and they can also tell us more about adjectives and past participles).

1 Find the adverbs in paragraph B on page 75 that describe the verbs **ask** and **take up**. Do you think they make the text clearer?

Can you think of two adverbs to add to the other two verbs that are underlined?

GRAMMAR

Forming adverbs

- Most adverbs are formed by adding *-ly* to an adjective, e.g.

  awful – awfully   *bad – badly*
  bright – brightly   *smart – smartly*

- If the adjective ends in *-e*, the *-e* is replaced with *-ly*. If it ends in *-y*, the *-y* is replaced with *-ily*, e.g.

  simple – simply   *happy – happily*
  terrible – terribly   *tidy – tidily*

- There are some irregular adverbs which you need to learn, e.g.

  good – well   *fast – fast*

- Some adverbs are not formed from adjectives, e.g. *very, too, so,* etc.
  These are often used with adjectives,
  e.g. It's *so hot* in this room.
  Or they modify other adverbs,
  e.g. The old man was driving *too slowly*.

- To make a negative adverb, you may need to add a prefix such as *un-, dis-, mis-, in-, im-, ir-* to the word, e.g.

  ir + regular + ly

- Some adverbs do not have a negative form (e.g. you can't say *uncleverly*) so you need to choose a word that has an *opposite meaning* to *cleverly*, such as *stupidly*.

- Adverbs can also be used with past participles, e.g.

  The picture was *badly damaged*.
  The club is *(very) well organised*.

- Certain adverbs go well with certain adjectives and others don't, e.g.

  I'm *absolutely freezing*. ✓
  I'm *highly freezing*. ✗

✓ Test tip

If you use adverbs well it will improve your writing, but you need to consider a) which is the best adverb to use, b) how to form the adverb, c) where to place it.

2 Change these words into adverbs. Can you add a prefix to the adverbs to make negative adverbs? If not, can you think of another adverb that has the opposite meaning?

	adverb	opposite
helpful	helpfully	unhelpfully
a expected		
b rapid		
c wide		
d happy		
e deliberate		
f usual		
g final		
h angry		
i good		

3 Use adverbs from the table in exercise 2 to complete these sentences.

  a The hairdresser .... cut off more hair than she meant to.
  b Amanda's friends .... offered to drive her to the airport.
  c The woman knew that her son was .... hiding something.
  d While writing her essay, Lily found that she was .... running out of ideas.
  e Mark arrived .... at his cousins' house and found that they weren't there.
  f Peter's essay was not .... written.
  g Mobile phones are .... used by young people.
  h My brother was .... cheerful this morning!

Note how the adverb comes *before* a single verb but *between* an auxiliary verb and its participle.

4 Describe each of these situations using a verb and an appropriate adverb.

knock over

kick

drive through

pick up

Academic and General Training Writing Task 2: Paragraph building

When you write your answer to Task 2, you need to write paragraphs that contain main ideas and supporting points.

1 **What is the topic and main idea of the paragraph opposite?**

2 **The writer of this paragraph gradually builds on the main idea by including supporting points. Can you identify the supporting points?**

3 **Look at this extract from a comic book. What are the advantages of reading about Einstein in this way? Discuss the question with a partner.**

4 **Follow the steps below and write *one* paragraph that answers the following question: 'Why do people enjoy reading cartoons?'**

  ▶ Identify three reasons why you think people like reading cartoons.

  ▶ Then, think of an example that illustrates *one* of the reasons.

  ▶ Write a sentence or two that explains the topic (cartoons) and main idea (why people like reading them).

  ▶ Give the three reasons for your main idea and, when appropriate, add your example.

  ▶ Write a final sentence that re-states your main idea in a different way.

Read your partner's paragraph. What approach has he or she taken to listing the supporting points?

Supporting your main ideas

In Writing Task 2 it is important to explain and give reasons for the points in your paragraphs. Otherwise, your paragraphs will look like lists.

5 **Read this first draft of a paragraph. It contains no grammar mistakes but it could be better. Then answer the questions below.**

> These days, there are many books for children to choose from and this has encouraged them to read for pleasure. Children enjoy reading because it is an independent activity. [*] In addition, it gives them a good opportunity to use their imagination. [*] Lastly, they use books to help them understand the world better. [*] All in all, children really like books.

  a What is the topic and main idea, and what are the supporting points?
  b Improve the paragraph by adding another sentence after each asterisk.
  c Can you improve the content of the final sentence?

The writer who works in an office is, in many ways, in a better environment than the writer who works from home. Well-run offices can be supportive places where staff can give and receive feedback on their work. This kind of assistance can be very comforting. In addition, as their colleagues are in the same field of work, there is a general appreciation of the stresses of the job. This leads to greater understanding when things go wrong. Overall, it seems it is healthier to write in an office than it is to write alone at home.

6 **Write a paragraph with the main idea 'Nowadays, people have no time for reading'. Include at least two supporting points, and try to write more than one sentence on each of them.**

Step up to **IELTS SPEAKING** *PART 3*

Giving relevant answers

After you have given your talk, listen carefully as the examiner introduces the first topic area.
Make sure you have understood, and decide how the examiner is expecting you to respond.

Step 1

Re-write the examiner's question below in your own words, in the thought bubble.
Use one of these words: *compare*, *describe*, *explain*, *predict*, *suggest*, *recommend*.

> *Let's talk about why people decide to write a book. What sort of reasons do you think people have for writing novels?*

> She wants me to ....
> ....
> ....

Step 2

Decide on your view.
In this case, do you think there is
a one main reason?
b more than one reason?
c no particular reason?

Step 3

Quickly think of some key vocabulary related to the topic and your focus.
• **Which of these words do you think would be useful in answering the question about writing novels?**

> ambition   knowledge   sell
> experience   financial   boring
> title   personal   bookshop

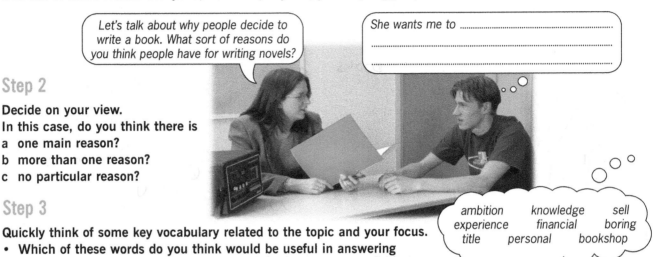

Step 4

Begin your answer with a clear statement that directly addresses the question and that opens the discussion.

• **Read these three responses and decide which is likely to lead into a discussion and allow you to use the vocabulary you know.**

> **OPENING THE DISCUSSION**
> Well, in my view there's one main …
> I think it depends on …
> It's difficult to say because I've never /
> I don't … but …
> I think there are a number of …

a *I don't know because I don't know anyone who's written a book.*

b *I think they need money so that's why they do it.*

c *If you ask writers, they all say something different.*

• **In pairs, re-phrase each of the answers a, b, and c by using one of the 'Opening the discussion' phrases above.**

• **Now try answering the question yourself by giving your own view.**

Step 5

The examiner will develop the topic by asking further questions that encourage you to support your ideas.

• **Ask your partner to support the view they gave in Step 4.**

> *What personal qualities do you think a writer needs to have?*

> *Could you ever write a novel?*

Step 6

The examiner will continue the discussion by asking some questions on another related topic. Here are some examples. Use the steps above to discuss these questions with your partner.

Now listen to the recording of a model Part 3 of the Speaking test.

> Do you think newspapers are a good source of information? Why? / Why not?
> How often do you read a newspaper?
> Should newspapers contain illustrations? Why? / Why not?

IELTS Test practice

SPEAKING TEST

Part 1

 Ask and answer the following questions.

a
> What are you studying at the moment?
> How long have you been studying it?
> Do you enjoy it? Why?
> Are there any other subjects you would like to study?

b
> How did you first learn to read?
> What did you prefer reading as a child?
> Have your reading habits changed since you were a child?

c

> When did you last go on holiday?
> Where did you go?
> How did you get there?
> What did you enjoy most?

d
> What is the most popular food in your country?
> Where do people buy it?
> How is it cooked?
> Do you think most people would like it? Why?

Part 2

 Give a 1–2 minute talk on this topic.

> Describe something that you have written that you are proud of.
> You should say
> – where and when you wrote it
> – why you wrote it
> – what it was about
> and explain why you were particularly proud of it.

Part 3

Discuss the following topics.

> **Writing versus technology**
> What effect have computers had on the way we write?
> What are the advantages/disadvantages of e-mail?
> Will writing remain an important skill in the future?
>
> **Writing and communication**
> How would you compare written and verbal communication? Are they different?
> Why do many companies/organisations rely on written communication?
> What are the features of 'good' writing?

Remember!

- First, you will answer questions about yourself. Then, you will give a 1–2 minute talk on a topic chosen by the examiner. Third, you will discuss some more abstract topics related to your talk by giving your views and opinions.
- The examiner will be assessing your language NOT your views but you should always stick to the topic.

Approach

- In the first part, try to add a little extra information to each answer, but don't overdo it and talk for too long.
- In the second part, use the one-minute preparation time to note down the main points of your talk before you give it. Try to keep going but don't rush yourself and don't worry if you need to pause. The examiner will wait for you to continue.
- In the third part, try to develop your ideas and take the opportunity to show the examiner what you can do. But keep to the topic.
- In all parts of the test:
- speak clearly – not too fast or too slowly – and link your ideas
- be adventurous with vocabulary and structures
- pronounce words clearly and use intonation and facial expression.

Down to Earth

Part 3: Discussing abstract topics

You will have to discuss an abstract topic in Part 3 of the Speaking test. This means you will need to offer an opinion on the topic and be able to support your point of view.

To get going

1 **Match these pictures to the 'green' topics a–h.**

a water management
b logging
c endangered species
d genetically modified crops
e rubbish and waste management
f environmental damage
g bushfires
h population

Pronunciation check

The sound /pr/

2 **Many words in English begin with two consonants. Listen and repeat these words and sentences after the recording.**

prevent   protect   produce   prevention
protection   production

Notice how the first syllable is weak, i.e. not stressed.

We need to prevent pollution.
We should protect our planet.
We need to produce more food.

The sound /v/

3 **Make the sound /v/ by putting your top teeth against your bottom lip.
Listen and repeat these words and sentences after the recording.**

involve   conserve   involvement
conservation   environment

We need to get involved.
We need more community involvement.
We must conserve our food.
The key is conservation.

Suggesting solutions

4 **Ask and answer questions about the topics in exercise 1. Use the Question starters and Useful words to help you.**

What can we do to stop people from wasting water?

How can we do this?

I think we should encourage people to recycle their water.

Maybe we should introduce legislation to make recycling compulsory.

QUESTION STARTERS

How can we stop …?
What do you think …?
Should …?
Why do you think …?
What should governments
   do about …?
How would you …?

Useful words

to prevent	prevention
to protect	protection
to reduce	reduction
to pollute	pollution
to produce	production
to legislate	legislation
to introduce	introduction
to involve	involvement
to encourage	encouragement
to dispose of	disposal
to recycle	recycling

IELTS LISTENING SECTION 3

Dealing with mixed question types

Section 3 is a conversation between two or more speakers on a topic related to academic work or study. Like all the other sections it can contain a variety of question types.

To get going

Look at questions a, b and c below and the handwritten notes. Then listen to an interview about a recycling project at Taronga Zoo, Sydney, and answer the questions in your own words, using **NO MORE THAN THREE WORDS AND/OR A NUMBER** for each answer.

Resource?
Power, timber, paper,
food, water, rubbish

recycling = using again

a What resource are they recycling at the Taronga Zoo?
....

b Where is the resource being re-used?
....

c How much money has already been saved?
....

What part of the zoo?

Note the tense.

Make sure your answers fit the instructions or they will be marked wrong. Look at these answers and decide what is wrong with them.

a water from animals' cages
b lawns
c 70,000

Now do the IELTS Listening tasks following the Steps.

Questions 1–3: Short answers

Step 1

Look at questions 1–3 and highlight the key words.

Step 2

Make your own notes to help you anticipate the answers.

Step 3

Listen to the interview about a campaign to clean up the environment and write answers to the questions.

Test tip

In the test, use a highlighter pen to highlight key words.

IELTS LISTENING TASK

Questions 1–3

Answer the questions below.

*Write **NO MORE THAN THREE WORDS** for each answer.*

1 In which country did 'Clean Up the World' first get going?
....

2 What was the first objective of the organisation?
....

3 At the local level, what *particular* issue is important?
....

Question 4: Selecting words from a list

In some Listening questions you will have to pick some words from a list. You may not hear the exact words which are listed so you need to be able to recognise a similar meaning.

Step 1

Read the instruction at the top of question 4 carefully.

Step 2

Note the key word 'activities'.

Step 3

Note the exact number of activities that you have to pick.

Step 4

Try to understand all the words in the list. If there are some words you don't know, try guessing their meaning.

Step 5

 Listen to the second part of the interview and answer question 4.

Listen again and make a note of the exact words used on the recording. Notice how they are slightly different from the words in the list.

Questions 5–10: Multiple choice and matching

In 'matching' questions you will be given some words in a box to match to a list.

Step 1

Read the multiple choice question, question 5.

Step 2

Look at questions 6–10 and read the words in the box. If you don't know the meaning of some of them, try to guess.

Step 3

If appropriate, highlight any key words. Can you think of a synonym for these words? e.g. *study = research*

Step 4

 Listen again and answer questions 5–10.

Question 4

4 *Choose* **THREE** *letters A–G.*

Which **THREE** *'Clean up the World' activities are mentioned?*

A Rubbish collecting
B Environmental walks
C Musical events
D Radio and TV appearances
E Cycling rallies
F Contacting politicians
G Advertising campaigns

 Test tip

You have to choose three activities here, but you will only get one mark as this is considered to be one question. If you choose fewer than three or more than three you will lose the mark.

You only need to write the letters A to G on your answer sheet.

Question 5

*Choose the correct letter, **A, B,** or **C.***

5 Which is the newest member country of 'Clean Up the World'?

A Algeria

B Vietnam

C Armenia

Questions 6–10

Match each area to the correct issue.

*Choose your answers from the box and write the letters **A–G** next to questions 6–10.*

6 America ....
7 Western Europe ....
8 Australia ....
9 Hawaii ....
10 Gulf of Mexico ....

Issues	
A Albatross study	**E** Fishing rights
B Drinks cans	**F** Plastic bags
C Automobile tyres	**G** Rubbish bins
D Dead zone	

 Test tip

There are more options A–H than you need. You only need to write the letter, and not the full answer, on your answer sheet.

Academic and General Training Writing Task 2: Balancing your views

Sometimes when you write a Task 2 answer, you do not have a clear-cut opinion. You may feel there are a number of points of view which you would like to express.

1 With a partner, discuss the following topic.

Shipping companies that allow oil to spill into the oceans should be made to pay for all the clean-up costs. They should also receive heavy fines.

Discuss both these views.

Then complete the paragraph using suitable words or phrases from the box.

a .... it seems reasonable to ask shipping companies to pay for the clean-up costs of damage they have caused, this is not always as easy as it sounds. b .... it may not be possible to say who is to blame, and c .... they may be unwilling to accept responsibility. Some companies have been successfully prosecuted, d .... it often takes years to get a result. e .... fines f .... , sometimes the companies simply don't have the money, g .... it is a waste of time chasing them.

> ✓ **Test tip**
>
> If there are two parts to a question, you must answer both parts. You will find more practice on this in Unit 13.

Useful expressions

Although … / Even though …
As far as the question of … is concerned
For one thing … for another
but
so

2 Now look at what a supermarket manager and two customers have to say about supermarket plastic bags. Do you agree with any of them? If so, why?
Write a sentence expressing each person's opinion.

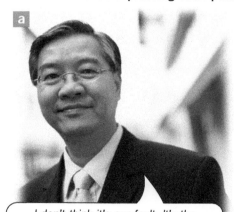

a

I don't think it's our fault. It's the customers' problem. Why can't they dispose of their bags in a sensible way?

b *The supermarkets are to blame because they give us too many bags. They should stop doing this.*

c *I take my own bag to the supermarket. That way I don't have any bags to get rid of.*

a According to ....
b The woman thinks ....
c ....

3 Now combine the three points of view above to form one paragraph which answers this question: *Who should be responsible for the disposal of supermarket plastic bags?* You can use words from the box to help balance your ideas.

Useful expressions

Some people think …
Others argue that …
In my view …

WRITING

4 Match the raw material for which these animals are hunted to the pictures below.

a fur
b feathers
c shell
d ivory
e skin
f oil

5 Not everyone agrees about whether or not we should hunt animals.
Imagine what these people have to say on the subject. Try to come up with three different
points of view.

6 Write a paragraph balancing the views discussed in exercise 5 and which answers the
question: *Is it ever justifiable to hunt wild animals in their natural environment?*

GRAMMAR

> *stop* + *-ing* verb and *stop/prevent someone from* + *-ing* verb
>
> Notice the different use of the verbs *stop* and *prevent* in the sentences below.
>
> a I *stopped smoking* ten years ago.
> b The government *stopped providing* free school lunches.
> c The police *stopped* me *from entering* the building.
> d The fire *prevented* us *from using* the elevator.
>
> In sentences a and b the subject of the verb stops himself/herself.
> In sentences c and d the subject of the verb stops another person from doing something.

7 Now complete the sentences below using either the verb *stop* or *prevent* with an
appropriate form of the words in brackets.

a Be quiet and ....
(talk)
b The bad weather ....
(us / go / to the beach)
c The customs officer ....
(me / import / the wooden fruit bowl)
d We're trying to ....
(people / trade / in ivory)
e The green parties want to ....
(people / destroy / the environment)
f The company ....
(pay / tax / ten years ago)

IELTS Test practice

LISTENING Section 3

Questions 1–3

List **THREE** of John Gould's professions.

*Write **NO MORE THAN THREE WORDS** for each answer.*

1 ....

2 ....

3 ....

Questions 4–6

Complete the table below.

*Write **NO MORE THAN THREE WORDS** for each answer.*

Date	Event
1804	Gould was born
1820s	Worked as a gardener and then in a **4** ....
1838	Sailed to Australia
1838–40	Gould **5** .... and .... many new species
1840	Returned to England
1848	Published book entitled **6** ....

Questions 7–10

*Write **NO MORE THAN THREE WORDS AND/OR A NUMBER** for each answer.*

7 What part of the animals could be effectively reproduced using lithography?

....

8 What did Gould use to make the first drawing on limestone?

....

9 How were the prints coloured?

....

10 How many prints did Gould produce of each picture?

....

Remember!

- Section 3 is always a dialogue. It may have two parts with a short break between these.
- The topic for Section 3 is always based on a study area and will involve a discussion between two or three speakers.
- The questions here are listing, table completion and short-answer questions but you could get any IELTS question type here.
- You will *never* need to write more than three words.

Approach

- Before the recording begins, read the questions carefully and try to predict the type of words you will need.
- Listen carefully at the start so that you know who the different speakers are.

Safe as houses

IELTS LISTENING *SECTION 4*

Section 4 is always a talk or mini-lecture related to academic work or study. Note-taking and short-answer questions are common, but other question types may also be used.

To get going

1 **Look at the words in the box and categorise them under the four headings below.**

place where you live	parts of a building	building materials	people
apartment	balcony	brick	architect

apartment architect balcony brick builder carpenter column concrete door dwelling engineer flat floor home house landlord level mud neighbour roof room skyscraper stairs steel stilts stone tenant tile verandah wall window wood

2 **Now look at these different types of building and decide where you might find them. What are the special features of each of these buildings? Select one and describe it to your partner.**

Example: *House **a** is a large brick house with two floors and quite a lot of windows. It has a garden and looks as if it belongs in a cool climate; for instance it could be in northern Europe or America.*

stilt house

chalet

In Section 4 you usually have about 45 seconds to look at the questions before the recording starts. Use this time to notice how the questions are organised and think about what the answers might be. This will help you to know what to listen for.

Step up to IELTS LISTENING

Step 1

Read the questions opposite to get an idea of the topic and layout of the first set of questions. Then listen to the first part of a lecture about the history of building and architecture and answer questions 1–6 using no more than THREE words.

✓ **Test tip**

You will hear all the answers on the recording. Don't write things that you don't hear on the recording even if you think they are correct.

Topic vocabulary can be tested in a number of ways in the IELTS test. One way is to ask you to recognise diagrams or pictures and their features.

Step 2

Look at questions 7 and 8 and the photos.

What type of words can you expect to hear on the recording? Can you predict the answers?

Step 3

Now look at questions 9 and 10.

What sort of words do you expect to hear for each set of pictures?

Listen to the second part of the lecture and answer questions 7–10.

IELTS LISTENING TASK

Questions 1–6

Complete the notes below. Write **NO MORE THAN THREE WORDS** *for each answer.*

Caves provided shelter from
– dangerous animals and **1** ....

Over the centuries, buildings became more
– practical as well as **2** ....

Architecture aims to provide a safe and healthy environment for people to
– live and **3** ....

The three main principles of architecture are
– function – **4** ....
– artistic expression

Architectural style is determined by:

Physical and mental state of **5** .... the people ....

Availability **6** .... of materials ....

Questions 7 and 8

In which country would you see these houses?

Choose your answers from the box and write the letters **A–E** *next to questions 7–8.*

Countries
A Greece
B Egypt
C Sweden
D Switzerland
E Vietnam

7 ....   8 ....

Questions 9 and 10

*Choose the correct letter, **A**, **B** or **C**.*

9 Which of these drawings shows a proper post and lintel?

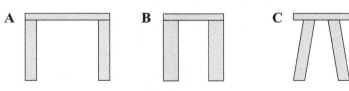

10 Which of these drawings shows a Roman arch?

SPEAKING

Speaking Part 3

Comparing and contrasting

In Part 3 you may be asked to make comparisons between different aspects of the topic.
You may feel that there are positive and negative points to discuss.

1 Look at the examiner's question below and the ideas which the student has.

Can you describe some of the benefits of living in an apartment, as opposed to a house?

- easy to maintain
- safe and secure
  BUT
- rather impersonal

Now link the student's ideas using this framework to create an answer.

> **Comparing**
> I think there are a number of good reasons for living in an apartment. For instance …
> And also …
> But, on the other hand …
> It really depends on …

> ✔ **Test tip**
> Be prepared for the examiner to ask a follow-up question such as *Why?* or *In what way?*

Supporting a view

You also need to be prepared to give a reason to support your views.

2 Read and answer the examiner's questions below giving reasons to support your answers. There are some ideas to help you but you can use your own ideas.

You've been talking about a building you particularly like. Can you suggest reasons why governments like to create impressive buildings … such as a national art gallery or a huge sports stadium?

Can you see any disadvantages to doing this? Why?

As far as I can see, one reason why governments put up impressive buildings is so that … Another is …

- to impress overseas visitors
- governments and famous people wanting to be remembered
- cultural needs
BUT
- not always good, e.g. ugly civic buildings

3 Ask and answer these questions.
a How does *your* home differ from your grandparents' home?
b What are the advantages of living in the countryside as opposed to a city?
c In the last century, we built more and more skyscrapers. Why do you think that was?
d These days we see more 'green' buildings that are environmentally friendly. What do you think is the reason for this?

> ✔ **Test tip**
> Remember to use some of the other expressions you know to introduce and link ideas, such as *while/whereas, because, so that*, etc.

> ✔ **Test tip**
> Contractions are very common in spoken English, but it is better not to use them in your written work unless you are writing an informal letter.

> **Useful expressions**
> I think that's fine as long as …
> It's important to make sure …
> Sometimes, they just want to …
> Quite often, I think they …

Pronunciation check: contractions

4 Many words are joined together in spoken English. Say the following contractions.

it's   I'll   I'd   that's   we'll   he'd
there's   you'll   you'd   she's   they'll   we'd

Do you know the 'long forms' of these words? Now say the following:
a I expect we'll see an increase …
b It's very hard to say …
c We'll have to see what happens.
d I'd rather live in a flat.
e There's no way of knowing for sure.

Step up to IELTS ACADEMIC AND GENERAL TRAINING WRITING *TASK 2*

Analysing the question

Before you start writing, you need to think about what the task is asking you to do. IELTS Writing tasks vary: there may be only one point of view that you have to discuss or there may be two parts to the question.

Tasks that have one focus

Some tasks consist of a single statement and you have to give your view on it. This means that you may agree, disagree or do both. You should decide what your view is before you start planning your answer.

> ✔ **Test tip**
>
> In Writing Task 2 you will have to give an opinion, backed up by reasons and some personal experience. You will lose marks if you do not do this. However, there is no 'correct' answer.

> Architects are responsible for the ugly buildings ...

Step 1: Understanding the stated point of view

- **In pairs, discuss the statements opposite. If you don't know all the words, try to guess their meaning. Re-write the statements in your own words.**

- **Do you agree or disagree with the statements? Perhaps you agree in part.**

- **Do you have any personal experience to help you? Try to justify your opinion by giving one or two reasons to your partner.**

> A *Architects are to blame for the construction of many ugly buildings in our cities today.*
>
> *To what extent do you agree or disagree with this statement?*

> B *In the past, buildings reflected the culture of a society but today all modern buildings look alike.*
>
> *How true do you think this is?*

Step 2: Agreeing with the stated point of view

Take 10 minutes to do this task.

- **Pick one of the statements above that you agree with.**
- **Write three reasons why you agree.**
- **Write a paragraph based on one of the reasons. Your paragraph should contain at least three sentences. Refer to the words in the original statement and link your sentences to the central idea.**

> **Useful expressions**
>
> I think it is reasonable to say that …
> I also believe that …
> In addition, …
> While it may be true that …
> I also feel …
> Although some people argue that …
> overall, I believe …
> The most important thing is …

Step 3: Making a concession before you disagree

Making a concession means agreeing in part. If you do this at the beginning of your paragraph, it makes your argument sound more balanced.

- **Look at the other statement and find a reason to disagree with it. Write another paragraph justifying this view. It can be useful to agree in part at the beginning of the paragraph and then put forward an opposing point of view. Write at least three sentences.**

- **Check your paragraph to make sure that your main idea is clearly stated and supported by examples.**

Step up to IELTS ACADEMIC AND GENERAL TRAINING WRITING

Recognising the two parts within a task

Sometimes the Task 2 question will have two parts to it. You must answer both parts or you will lose marks.

Step 1

- Read the tasks opposite and highlight the key words in the statement and the question(s).
- Circle the two parts that you need to write about.
- Summarise the task for yourself in your own words.

Step 2

Write two paragraphs for Task B, putting forward a balanced point of view. Try to create a link between the ideas.

> A *Architects are mainly concerned with individual buildings rather than with the effect these buildings have on our cities as a whole.*
>
> *To what extent do you agree with this statement?*
>
> *How closely should architects work with town planning departments?*

> B *Some people argue that there is no point in preserving old buildings when land is so valuable in our cities. Others believe that old buildings are an important part of our heritage and should be preserved.*
>
> *Discuss both these views.*

Useful expressions

I tend to feel that …
In my opinion, it is …
We should consider whether …
It is useful to consider what effect … could have on …

Some people feel that …
It can be argued that …
It can be said that …

Tackling a full task

Take 40 minutes for this task.

- Look at the question opposite and note how it is set out. You should have some views on the topic already.

- Decide exactly what the question is asking you to do. How many parts does it have? What are they?

Make some notes using the framework below to organise them and then write your answer.

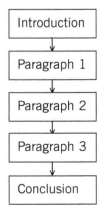

Introduction
↓
Paragraph 1
↓
Paragraph 2
↓
Paragraph 3
↓
Conclusion

Time limit

Body of question in bold

You should spend about 40 minutes on this task.

Present a written argument or case to an educated reader with no specialist knowledge of the following topic.

> ***In the past, buildings often reflected the culture of a society but today all modern buildings look alike and cities throughout the world are becoming more and more similar.***
>
> ***What do you think is the reason for this, and is it a good thing or a bad thing?***

You should use your own ideas, knowledge and experience and support your arguments with examples and relevant evidence.

You should write at least 250 words.

What is your personal experience?

Word limit

IELTS Test practice

ACADEMIC WRITING Task 2

(This task is also suitable practice for the General Training Module. See page 73.)

You should spend about 40 minutes on this task.

Present a written argument or case to an educated reader with no specialist knowledge of the following topic.

> ***In many major cities of the world, you will find large public buildings, both new and old.***
>
> ***Discuss the advantages and disadvantages of such buildings.***
>
> ***How important is it for a country to construct impressive public buildings when houses are what is really required?***

You should use your own ideas, knowledge and experience and support your arguments with examples and relevant evidence.

You should write at least 250 words.

✔ Test tip

If you do not divide your answer into paragraphs, you will lose marks.

Remember!

- There are two tasks in the Writing test and Task 2 carries more marks. So you need to spend more time on this task.
- In Task 1 you get information to write about. In Task 2 you need to give your personal opinions on the topic.
- There is no 'correct' answer. To get a good mark, give your opinion, then give reasons for it and examples.
- You get marks for good grammar and a wide vocabulary, but also for giving a clear message.
- You should show that you can write formal, academic English.

Approach

- Read the question carefully and decide how many points need addressing.
- Make some quick notes with three or four main ideas, each of which can be developed into a paragraph.
- Begin your answer with an introductory paragraph outlining the topic but do not copy word for word from the question as language that has been 'lifted' will not be marked.
- Divide your answer into three or four paragraphs, each one containing one of your main ideas. For each statement, try to give either an example or some evidence to support the idea.
- Finish with a concluding paragraph that summarises your main point.
- Leave time at the end to check your answer for errors in grammar, spelling and punctuation.

UNIT 14 *On the face of it*

Expressing feelings and opinions

1 Look at the pictures of people's faces. Discuss how they look and how you think they feel. Use an adverb (*slightly/pretty/fairly*) to help you be precise. Do you agree with each other?

Useful words

pleased amused
excited
flattered
shocked surprised horrified
angry annoyed irritated
disappointed sad
calm relieved
hurt offended
suspicious curious
thoughtful
nervous worried frightened terrified
uncomfortable uneasy anxious
confused uncertain
indifferent unconcerned undecided
bored uninterested fed up

2 Say how you *would feel* if someone said the following to you.

Example: *If someone said, 'You look nice,' I would feel/be flattered.*

a *Would you like to give a presentation to the class next week?*

b *Let's go and see that new horror film.*

d *You're the best cook I know.*

c *I'm afraid you didn't do very well in your recent exam.*

e *Why don't you do more exercise?*

Can you explain why? Try making an appropriate face to go with the feeling.

3 Choose four of the feelings in the 'Useful words' box and think of something that someone might say to you that would produce that feeling. Write down the four sentences.

4 Our opinions result from the way we feel and think about a topic.

Ask and express your feelings about the following topics using the Question and Sentence starters. Add a sentence or two that supports your views.

Example: A: *How do you feel about smoking in public places?*
B: *I feel rather undecided about it. On the one hand, I think people should be free to smoke if they want to, but on the other hand, they ought to consider other people.*

a Smoking in public places b Teenage marriage c Eating meat d Fashion magazines e Single-sex schools

GRAMMAR

should / ought to

We often use *should* and *ought to* when we are expressing opinions about how we think people should behave or we are making a recommendation that we think is right for the future.

For example: I think smoking *should* be banned.
People *ought to* think more carefully about what they eat.

Must is too strong and too certain.

QUESTION STARTERS
How do you feel about …?
What are your views on …?

SENTENCE STARTERS
I feel very strongly that …
I'm rather concerned/worried about …
… makes me feel a bit …
I'm very much in favour of …
I don't have terribly strong views about …

Recognising feelings and identifying views

In any part of the Listening test you may have to answer questions on the speakers' feelings or views.
You need to recognise vocabulary related to feelings and note expressions that introduce an opinion.

1 Listen to some people talking and decide how each one feels (use adjectives from the box on page 92). Write the adjectives in the 'feeling' column.

2 Listen a second time and write down the words that the speaker uses to show how he or she feels.

3 Listen a third time and notice how they use intonation to help get the message across.

speaker	feeling	words used
1	disappointed	let down
2		
3		
4		
5		
6		

4 Listen to Amanda and Walid discussing smoking. Put a tick by the speaker who has the strongest feelings about the topic and write down the words that they use to describe their feelings.

	✓	words used
Amanda		
Walid		

5 Listen again and complete the sentence.
Walid doesn't like being with smokers when he is
A eating.
B walking.
C socialising.

6 Listen to a young woman talking about the topic of marriage. She discusses three different views on marriage. Complete the table as you listen.

	words used
other people's views	in favour of marriage
her parents' views	
her own views	

✓ Test tip

Listen out for signals like:
I think that …
In my view …
I would argue that …
It seems to me that …

They tell you that the speaker is about to express a viewpoint.

7 Answer the question. How does the speaker feel about marriage?
A She thinks she will get married soon.
B She is uncertain whether she will ever marry.
C She fears that her parents will force her to marry.

Multiple-choice questions often test feelings and views. In Part 3 of the Listening test, you hear two or
more speakers discussing a topic related to work or study. Often the speakers exchange views as they talk.

8 Take 30 seconds to underline any key words in the questions below, including those that focus on feelings or views.

1 The students think that their project is
   A unoriginal.
   B uninteresting.
   C unusual.

2 What does Hiba say about her teenage life?
   A It was like most other people's.
   B Some of it was disappointing.
   C She didn't enjoy it.

3 Ahmed suggests that they write about
   A something they did alone.
   B a significant event.
   C an unhappy time.

4 How did Ahmed's father feel about his idea?
   A He thought it was crazy.
   B He realised it was useless.
   C He believed it was right.

5 How does Hiba feel about Ahmed's challenge?
   A pleased
   B envious
   C unconcerned

✓ Test tip

You always have some time to read the questions before you listen. Make sure you use this time wisely: re-phrase the question in your own mind and underline the key words that tell you what to listen out for.

9 Listen to a conversation between two students and answer the questions above.

Dealing with research-based texts

A lot of IELTS Academic reading passages are about research. Often these passages describe a research process and provide information on the method, the data and the results.

First reading

1 Answer the questions.

   a The title of this article is a well-known expression. Do you know what it means?

   b What does the subheading tell you about the content of the article?

2 Take no more than 10 minutes to read through the article. To help you follow the line of development, complete the notes in the right-hand margin.

Face to Face

Malcolm Gladwell reports on the art – or is it science? – of face reading

All of us read faces. When someone says, 'I love you', we look into that person's eyes to judge his or her sincerity. When we meet someone new, we often pick up on subtle signals, so that, even though he or she may have talked in a normal and friendly manner, afterwards, we say, 'I don't think he liked me' or 'I don't think she's very happy'. We easily distinguish complex differences in facial expression.

   The face is such an extraordinarily efficient instrument of communication that there must be rules that govern the way we interpret facial expressions. But what are those rules? And are they the same for everyone? In the 1960s, a young psychologist named Paul Ekman began to study facial expression, and he discovered that no one knew the answers to those questions. Ekman went to see an anthropologist called Margaret Mead and suggested to her that he travel around the world to find out whether people from different cultures agreed on the meaning of different facial expressions. Mead *was unimpressed*. Like most social scientists of her day, she believed that expression was culturally determined – that we simply used our faces according to a set of learned social conventions.

   Ekman *was undaunted*; he began travelling to places like Japan, Brazil and Argentina, carrying photographs of men and women making a variety of distinctive faces. Everywhere he went, people agreed on what those expressions meant. But he wondered whether people in the developed world had all picked up the same cultural rules from watching the same movies and television shows. So he set out again, this time making his way through the jungles of Papua New Guinea, to the most remote villages, and he found that the tribesmen there had no problem interpreting the expressions either. This may not sound like much of a breakthrough. But in the scientific climate of the time, it was a revelation. Ekman had established that expressions were the universal products of evolution. There were fundamental lessons to be learned from the face, if you knew where to look.

   If the face was part of a physiological system, he reasoned, the system could be learned. He set out to teach himself and was introduced to the face reading business by a man named Silvan Tomkins, possibly the best face reader of all time. Ekman's most memorable encounter with Tomkins took place in the late 1960s. Ekman had just tracked down 30,000 metres of film that had been shot by the virologist Carleton Gajdusek in the remote jungles of Papua New Guinea. Some of the footage was of a tribe called the South Fore, who were peaceful and friendly people. The rest was of the Kukukuku, who were hostile and murderous. Ekman was still working on the problem of whether human facial expressions were universal, and the Gajdusek film was invaluable. For six

---

The importance of

a............................ *in everyday communication*

↓

Ekmans's first research project: Does everyone use the same

b............................ *to interpret facial expressions?*

↓

Description of two research projects on the relationship between face reading and

c............................

↓

Introduction to Tomkins and the preparation of research material using

d............................ *of Papua New Guinea tribes*

↓

months, Ekman and his collaborator, Wallace Friesen, sorted through the footage. They cut extraneous scenes, focusing just on close-ups of the faces of the tribesmen, and when the cuts were finished, Ekman called in Tomkins.

The two men, protégé and mentor, sat at the back of the room, as faces flickered across the screen. Ekman had told Tomkins nothing about the tribes involved. At the end, Tomkins went up to the screen and pointed to the faces of the South Fore. 'These are a sweet gentle people, very indulgent, very peaceful,' he said. Then he pointed to the faces of the Kukukuku. 'This other group is violent, and there is lots of evidence to suggest murder.' Even today, a third of a century later, Ekman *cannot get over* what Tomkins did. Ekman recalls, 'He went up to the screen and, while we played the film backward in slow motion, he pointed out the particular bulges and wrinkles in the face that he was using to make his judgement. 'That's when I realised,' Ekman says, 'that I had to unpack the face.'

Ekman and Friesen decided that they needed to create a taxonomy* of facial expressions, so day after day, they sat across from each other and began to make every conceivable face they could. Soon, though, they realised that their efforts weren't enough. 'I met an anthropologist, Wade Seaford, and told him what I was doing, and he said, "Do you have this muscular movement?"' And it wasn't in Ekman's system because he had never seen it before. 'I had built a system based not on what the face can do, but on what I had seen. I *was devastated*. I realised that I had to learn the anatomy.'

The two then combed through medical textbooks that outlined each of the facial muscles, and identified every distinct muscular movement that the face could make. There were 43 such movements. Ekman and Friesen called them 'action units'. Then they sat across from each other again and began manipulating each action unit in turn, first locating the muscle in their mind and then concentrating on isolating it, watching each other closely as they did, checking their movements in a mirror and videotaping the movements for their records.

When each of those action units had been mastered, Ekman and Friesen began working action units in combination. The entire process took seven years. 'There are 300 combinations of two muscles,' Ekman says. 'If you add in a third muscle, you get over 4000. We took it up to five muscles, which is over 10,000 visible facial configurations.' Most of those 10,000 facial expressions don't mean anything, of course. They are the kind of nonsense faces that children make. But, by working through each action-unit combination, Ekman and Friesen identified about 3000 that did seem to mean something, until they had catalogued the essential repertoire of human emotion.

* a scientific list

Ekman shows surprise at Tomkins's ability to

e ....

....

↓

Description of how Ekman developed a

f ....

and why this wasn't good enough

↓

An explanation of how each **g** ....

was identified

↓

The production of the final collection of

h ....

....

If you form a quick overview of the development of the passage, you will find the questions easier because you will know which part of the passage to check for the answers.

3 Take no more than 7 minutes to do this IELTS-type summary.

*Complete the summary below using **NO MORE THAN THREE WORDS AND/OR A NUMBER** from the reading passage.*

Although we may not realise it, we **1** .... on a daily basis. In the 1960s, a psychologist named Paul Ekman decided to establish the **2** .... that govern how we do this. He first carried out his research using **3** .... which he took with him to different countries. By doing this, he discovered that there was no **4** .... link to the way we interpret expressions. But it was after his meetings with **5** .... that he began to create a list of facial expressions. By analysing every **6** .... that the face can make, he and his partner identified a total of **7** .... different facial expressions.

IELTS READING *MATCHING (PEOPLE)*

IELTS passages often present an argument and, in order to support the argument, the writer may make references to other experts. This is typical in academic writing. To show that you can understand the references, you may have to match the people to their opinions/actions or to facts that relate to them.

Step 1

 Take 1 minute to read through the IELTS task opposite and underline any key words in the statements.

 Test tip

As there are 7 questions and only 6 people, you will need to use at least one of the letters twice. There may also be some letters (people) that you do not use at all. Each question only has one answer.

Step 2

 Take 1 minute to scan the passage on pages 94–95 for all the names in the box and underline them.

Step 3

 Take 2 minutes.

- **Go to the part of the text where Ekman is mentioned for the first time.**

- **Now re-read statements 1–7 to see whether one of them matches any of the points in that part of the passage.**

IELTS READING TASK

Look at the following statements (Questions 1–7) and the list of people below.

Match each statement with the correct person.

NB *You may use any letter more than once.*

1 helped edit material for an experiment
2 introduced a factor that had been overlooked
3 is considered by some to be the most successful interpreter of facial expression
4 rejected the usefulness of an idea
5 realised that many areas of facial expression were unexplained
6 provided useful material for research
7 successfully distinguished characteristics from unknown faces

List of People
A Paul Ekman
B Margaret Mead
C Silvan Tomkins
D Carleton Gajdusek
E Wallace Friesen
F Wade Seaford

 Test tip

Note that the order of people in the list matches the order in which they occur in the text. You only need to write the letters A to F on your answer sheet.

---

there must be rules that govern the way we interpret facial expressions. But what are those rules? And are they the same for everyone? In the 1960s, a young psychologist named Paul Ekman began to study facial expression, and he discovered that no one knew the answers to those questions. ◄───

Same meaning as statement 5

Step 4

 Take 10 minutes to do the rest of the task.
Using the same procedure, move on to the next name – Margaret Mead – and see whether any of the statements (1–7) correspond to what is said about her.

Another type of matching task is classification. There is an example of this on page 111.

 Test tip

Some names (e.g. Ekman) occur in the passage more than once. Therefore, it is important that you underline every occurrence of a name and check the text around that name each time.

IELTS Test practice

SPEAKING TEST

Part 1

Ask and answer the following questions.

a

Where is your home town?
What type of building does your family live in?
How long has your family lived there?
What are the advantages of living there?

b

When did you first use a computer?
Do you think computers are bad for your health?
Which computer software do you use most?
What purpose did you last use a computer for?

c

What's the weather like in your home country?
How does wet weather make you feel?
Is it important to experience different types of weather?
What do you like to do in hot weather?

d

Have you ever been to a wedding? Where?
What clothes do people wear to weddings in your country?
What sort of gifts do guests buy for the couple?
How long does the wedding ceremony last?

Part 2

Give a 1–2 minute talk on this topic:

Describe a person (real or fictional) who you think has been lucky.
You should say
– who the person is
– how you know them
– what happened to them
and explain why you think this person was 'lucky'.

Re-read the Remember! box on page 79 to remind yourself about the Speaking test.

Assessment

The examiner will assess your ability to:

- link ideas and sentences
- develop your ideas, particularly in Part 3
- use a good range of vocabulary
- use a good range of grammatical structures
- pronounce clearly and use intonation and word stress effectively.

Tips

- Don't speak too quickly. It can make it difficult for the examiner to understand you.
- Don't mumble. Speak clearly or the examiner won't understand you.
- If you can't answer a question, tell the examiner. He or she will explain a word (Parts 1 and 2) or re-phrase the question (Part 3).
- Look at the examiner when you are speaking; this is not considered impolite.

Part 3

Discuss the following topics.

Luck and superstition
Do you think people in your country are superstitious?
Can you describe a typical superstition that they believe in?
Do you think people are less superstitious now than they used to be?
Will the future bring any new types of superstition?

Being 'lucky'
What activities do people take part in that are based on luck?
Is there a difference between luck and judgement?
Is it ever possible for people to create their own luck?
What sort of famous people would you describe as lucky?

READING

Following the writer's argument

When you first read a passage you should quickly form an overview of the main ideas/arguments. After that, you need to use the appropriate reading strategies to answer each set of questions.

First reading

1 **Read the title and the subheading of the article. What answer do you predict the writer will give to the question asked in the subheading?**

2 **Take 7 minutes to skim the passage and draw a simple flow diagram to show the main points in the writer's argument.**

3 **Write a two-sentence summary of the writer's main argument in your own words.**

✓ *Test tip*

Science and technology are popular topics in IELTS. You should read more about them to develop ideas.

Robots with emotion?

It seems possible to build a machine with an aspect of human intelligence, even a high IQ, but surely it will never have true emotional intelligence?

A You may shout at your computer – but how would you feel if it yelled back, or even burst into tears? Some experts believe that it is only a matter of time before truly intelligent computers and robots are created. But could a machine really think like a human?

B The traditional approach to Artificial Intelligence (AI) involves programming a computer with ever-increasing sophistication. In fact, there are already thousands of computers seeming to show some aspect of intelligence. Internet search engines, voice-recognition software, 'intelligent' clothing with built-in sensors that record bodily functions, expert systems that control manufacturing processes – all do important jobs as well as we could do them ourselves, and in many cases much faster.

C But the field of robotics shows how hard it really is to simulate intelligent human behaviour. The first domestic robot, the Aqua Queen – which cleans swimming pools, was launched in 1966 and there hasn't been much progress since then. The problem is navigation – a robot can't cope with a complex or changing environment; it gets lost very easily. A bigger challenge, however, is to get robots to do more than one task. Even the most intellectually-challenged human can do thousands of different things; a robot is usually dedicated to just one activity – vacuuming, lawn-mowing and so on. A multi-skilled robot would require a much higher level of intelligence, and that's not likely to happen for a long time.

D Perhaps the real hurdle in making computers and robots truly intelligent is to enable them to recognise and express emotion. In his book *Descartes' Error*, Antonio Damasio of the University of Iowa argues that emotion is essential for logical thought. For too long, he says, we have assumed that emotion clouds rationality, when in fact, the parts of the brain involved in both functions are linked in vital neuronal circuits.

E The emotional robot has long been a dream of science fiction. Over the last few years, computer scientists have been creating a range of animated agent faces – programs that generate images of human-like faces on a computer VDU. Researchers at the Massachusetts Institute of Technology have now constructed a robot called Kismet, which has a three-dimensional synthetic head with moveable eyelids, eyes and lips. When left alone, Kismet will look sad, but if a human enters the room, it smiles. If you are rough with it, an expression of fear develops. Kismet's inventors are now planning to provide the robot with a voice that can express emotion.

F Nevertheless, an 'emotional' robot – or computer – will also have to recognise emotions (this will simulate the key feature of emotional intelligence). Ifran Essa and Alex Pentland, two US computer scientists, have developed a program that enables a computer to recognise facial expressions corresponding to six basic emotions. When volunteers pretended to feel one of these emotions, the computer got it right 98 per cent of the time (better than most humans).

G However, AI pioneer Herbert Simon warns that robots must develop real emotions if they are to simulate human intelligence, because emotion is essential for survival and decision-making. So far, 'emotional' robots merely exhibit emotional behaviour. For real emotion – and real intelligence – they may have to evolve consciousness and self-awareness.

Step up to IELTS READING *LOCATING INFORMATION*

If the passage is divided into paragraphs, A, B, C, etc., you will either be tested on your understanding of the main idea of each paragraph (paragraph headings), or you will be asked to say which paragraph contains certain information (locating information). These are different types of question that need to be approached in different ways.

Step 1

Underline any key words in the questions (see Q1). Try to express each question in your own words so that you have a better understanding of what it means. Are you looking for key information or something that supports this, e.g. an example?

✓ Test tip

The NB is only given if at least two questions have the same answer. If there is no NB then all the answers will come from different paragraphs.

IELTS READING TASK

*This passage has seven paragraphs labelled **A–G**.*

Which paragraph contains the following information?

*Write the correct letters **A–G**.*

NB You may use any letter more than once.

1 a <u>comparison</u> between <u>human judgement</u> and that of a <u>robot</u>

2 examples of different types of intelligent technology

3 details of work on designing a robot with lifelike features

4 the name of a robot designed for home use

5 what is needed in order for robots to develop both emotion and intelligence

6 the reason why robots are generally used in one place

7 the rejection of a well established argument

Step 2

Skim through paragraph A on the opposite page and then skim through the set of questions. Do any questions correspond to information in paragraph A? If so, make a note of this. (Paragraph A is very short and simply introduces the idea of intelligent robots. None of the questions matches this.)

Step 3

Go on to paragraph B. As shown below, use your reading skills to identify the topic and the main and supporting ideas in the paragraph.

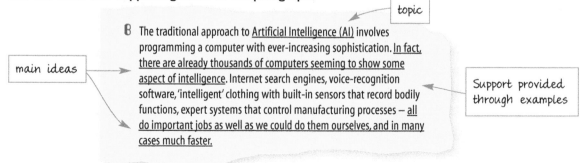

topic

main ideas

B The traditional approach to <u>Artificial Intelligence (AI)</u> involves programming a computer with ever-increasing sophistication. <u>In fact, there are already thousands of computers seeming to show some aspect of intelligence.</u> Internet search engines, voice-recognition software, 'intelligent' clothing with built-in sensors that record bodily functions, expert systems that control manufacturing processes – <u>all do important jobs as well as we could do them ourselves, and in many cases much faster.</u>

Support provided through examples

Re-read the questions noting the key words you have underlined. Does paragraph B relate to any of the questions?

Step 4

When you have decided, go on to paragraph C. Take 8 minutes to work through the rest of the questions.

In passages that present an argument or case, the writer often refers to other experts in the area. You may be tested on your understanding of this in other IELTS questions, e.g. matching (see page 96).

WRITING

Referring back

Referencing involves using words like this, these, who, which, such, *etc. It will avoid repetition and help your ideas to flow. The examiner will check your use of referencing in both writing tasks.*

1 Read the following description and underline any reference words or phrases.

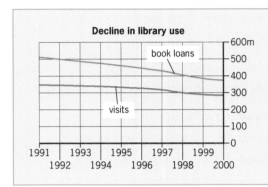

This graph shows the change in library use between 1991 and 2000. During this period, there was a gradual fall in the number of people who visited libraries and the number of books which were taken out on loan. This decline was more significant for book loans, which fell from 500 million in 1991 to just under 400 million in 2000. In comparison with this, general library visits fell from 350 million to 300 million over the same period. There was a slight levelling off for both in the last year of the decade.

2 Complete these sentences with the correct reference word (*this*, *these*, *it*, *which*, *who*, *there*, *such*).

This chart shows the reasons why people go to the library. The main reason is to borrow books. Just under 80 per cent of people visit for (a) .... purpose and (b) .... is by far the most significant reason. Thirty per cent of visitors go to the library to browse and 20 per cent go (c) .... to find information. (d) .... are the three most popular reasons for visiting. There are also people (e) .... visit the library to borrow CDs, videos and cassettes, although (f) .... visitors represent only a small percentage. And then there are a small number of other reasons, (g) .... include studying and seeing an exhibition.

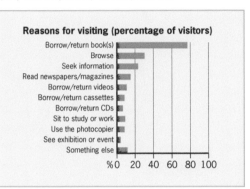

3 'This' is a useful way of referring back to a noun, e.g. *this argument*, *these ideas*. Complete the sentences with *this* or *these* + an appropriate noun.

Example: Some people state that genetically modified food is perfectly safe.
Unfortunately I don't agree with ....*this view*.........

a In the early 20th century, many buildings were designed to be beautiful *and* to last a long time, but .... gradually became less important.

b One large aerospace company has started research into a 250-seater sonic jet. Apparently, ... will fly just below the speed of sound.

c It is essential to teach children to swim. .... may save their lives in the future.

d Universities and colleges have an important social function. .... are the backbone of our education system.

e Some people believe you only need to study the night before an exam, but .... is not recommended.

f Scientists are looking at ways of growing human cells to repair damaged tissue. However, research of .... raises many ethical questions.

g Teachers are in favour of young children going to nursery school, claiming that .... helps them learn how to socialise with other children.

GRAMMAR

such (a/an) + noun

You can also use *such* to refer back to what you wrote. It adds more emphasis to what you say and it is more formal. Always use *a* or *an* if you use *such* with a singular countable noun, e.g.

Some people state that genetically modified food is perfectly safe. *Such an* argument is hard to believe when so little research has been done.

4 Complete the sentences by using the word in brackets in a 'such' phrase.

a Space travel is now a reality. However, ... was inconceivable a hundred years ago. (concept)

b My uncle believes that all boys of 18 should do military service, but I don't agree with .... (old-fashioned view)

c The early sailors had to navigate without GPS and radar. Amazingly, they managed without .... (instruments)

d Smoking is not allowed in public buildings in Australia. And in fact .... is actually forbidden by law. (behaviour)

5 Read this essay and make the improvements suggested by the marker.

a) Avoid this repetition

b) Use a reference word + noun

e) Insert a noun phrase that refers back to your examples

f) Wrong reference word

In the 21st century, our lives seem to be dominated by technology. In fact, technology has become the most powerful influence over life because everything that we do is related to technology. The house we live in, the food we eat, the office we work in and the exercise equipment that keeps us fit – all depend on technology in one way or another.

Perhaps we should consider what would happen if all the technology we use began to break down. We would certainly appreciate technology more if it happened. Take for example the home. It contains things like a fridge, washing machine, vacuum cleaner, etc. Without these, we would have to spend a lot more time in the home and so we would have less time to do other, possibly more interesting, things. So this makes life easier for us.

Similarly, when we go to work, we depend on computers to write reports and documents and we rely on e-mail for our day-to-day correspondence. In fact, technology is changing the workplace very rapidly. Things like video-conferencing, it is becoming more and more commonplace, mean that business people need fewer meetings, and international companies can cut down on overseas travel. Without these businesses would suffer.

It's true that technology can be irritating, time-consuming and rather impersonal. Although we often make complain about it, we should accept that it has transformed the way we live and hopefully it will continue to do so.

c) Wrong reference word

d) Join these sentences

g) Use 'such' + noun phrase

h) Use a reference word + 'complaints'

WRITING

SPEAKING

Talking about the future

*You will have to talk about the future in the Speaking test. Remember that in Parts 1 and 2, the topics are **familiar** and **personal**. In the Part 3 discussion, however, you will have to speculate or make predictions about **abstract** topics.*

1 Underline the verb forms in this conversation and then read the grammar box below.

a *What are you doing this weekend?*

b *I'm quite tired so I think I'll stay at home. What are you going to do?*

c *My sister's coming to stay. I think we'll probably go and see a film.*

GRAMMAR

The present continuous tense or *going to* forms are used when we are **certain** about the future – often because a plan has already been made or started.

When we make **predictions** about the future which are reasonably, but not completely, certain, we tend to use *think + will* or *think + going to*, e.g.

I *think* the democrats *are going to win* the election. We *think we'll take* our next holiday somewhere in South East Asia.

2 Ask and answer these questions.

a Where are you going on your next holiday?
b What type of person do you think you'll marry?
c Where do you think you'll be in ten years' time?
d How do you think you'll celebrate your next birthday?
e What are you planning to do after your studies?

Predicting and speculating

3 Look at these pictures and say what you think is going to happen next.

GRAMMAR

When making **predictions** about an **unreal** situation (i.e. something that may or may not happen) we use *would*, and if we are not certain, we can speculate about it using *might* or *could*. We still often use *I think* with these expressions, e.g.

How do you think people *would feel* about having a robot in their home?

– *I think* people *would feel* uneasy about having a robot in their home. (predicting)
– *I think* they *could feel* uneasy about it. (less certain – speculating)
– *I think* they *might feel* threatened by it. (less certain – speculating)

4 Underline the verb forms in these conversations.

Do you think anyone will ever invent a robot that can do all the housework?

Yes, I think it's very likely that they will.

How do you think this would affect people's lives?

Well, I can't really foresee any problems. I think it would give people a lot of extra time to do other things.

5 Discuss the topics below. If your partner doesn't give a very full answer, try to ask a follow-up question.

Do you think anyone will ever ...?

a ... successfully clone human beings?
b ... use computers to mark speaking tests?
c ... use robots to do medical operations?
d ... build holiday hotels in space?
e ... develop drugs that lengthen our lifespan?

Pronunciation check: word stress

6 Speakers of English often stress key information to make their meaning clearer. Listen to the recording of people speculating about topics a–e in exercise 5 and note the words and phrases that the speakers stress.

Useful expressions

I expect ...
I predict ... will lead to / result in
I foresee / I can't foresee any problems.
I suppose (*conceding*) ...

As far as I can see/tell ...
... in the foreseeable future
The result/outcome will/would be that ...
From what I've read/heard, it seems that ...

IELTS Test practice

LISTENING Section 4

Questions 1–4

*Label the diagram below. Write **NO MORE THAN THREE WORDS** for each answer.*

A Flight Simulator

Type of aircraft simulated:
1 ....

3 .... creates landscape

Hydraulic
2 ....

Instructor uses a
4 .... to train pilot

Questions 5–10

*Complete the notes below. Write **NO MORE THAN THREE WORDS**.*

Computers are run by 5 .... of software experts.

flight experts deal with
6 .... strength

navigation experts need to know the location of a storm

7 .... **experts** ensure a safe journey

Pilot training process

Learn how to enter data into the 8 ....

↓

Learn how the controls affect the 9 ....

↓

Learn to take off and fly

↓

Can fly with the title of 10 ....

SPEAKING

Expressing certainty or doubt

When you answer the examiner's questions you may wish to show that you can express certainty about your answers or that you have some doubts. There are many ways of doing this and they can improve what you say.

1 Answer the quiz questions.

Language Quiz

1 What does 'mother tongue' mean?
a) your mother's language   b) baby language   c) your native language

2 Approximately how many living languages are there in the world today?
a) 4,500   b) 10,000   c) 15,000

3 Approximately how many people in the world speak English as a first language?
a) 50 million   b) 350 million   c) 600 million

4 Outside Japan, where else is Japanese spoken by roughly 2 million people?
a) Brazil   b) Argentina   c) USA

5 For whom was the communication system known as Braille developed?
a) the deaf   b) the blind   c) the mentally handicapped

6 What nationality was the creator of the artificial language Esperanto?
a) French   b) Spanish   c) Polish

7 What do you call someone who studies the development and usage of language?
a) a polyglot   b) an interpreter   c) a linguist

8 Where would you hear Putonghuà spoken?
a) China   b) Mexico   c) Fiji

9 Which language has the most letters in its alphabet?
a) Khmer   b) Russian   c) English

10 When is language first thought to have appeared?
a) 7–10,000 years ago   b) 30–50,000 years ago   c) 100–200,000 years ago

2 Read the Grammar box on page 105 about indirect statements. Then discuss the quiz questions with a partner, saying what you think the answers are.

Example: *I'm sure the answer to Question 1 is (c). I'm not sure about Question 5. It could be (b).*

Use expressions from the box opposite.
Then check your answers on page 106.

Useful expressions from certain ... to less certain

I'm sure/certain that ...
I'm pretty sure/certain that ...
It seems likely that ...
I think that ...
It's hard to say whether ...
I don't really know whether ...

Indirect statements

Main clause		subject of subordinate clause	verb	
I don't know	if/whether	the answer	is	(a) or (b).
I'm not sure	if/whether	the statement	is	true or false.
We are discussing	whether (not *if* after *discuss*)	the government	should	spend more money on education.
I'm certain	(that)	Braille	was created	for the blind.

These expressions are also very useful when you speculate or make predictions about the future. Remember, if you are very certain, then you will probably use *will* or *going to*. If you are less certain, a modal verb such as *would*, *might* or *could* is better.

3 **Look at the pictures below and say what you think they mean or represent.**
Use expressions from the box below or from page 104.

Example: *I think **a** is probably an example of Egyptian writing, but I'm not sure. It looks as if it means …*

Were you predicting or speculating?

Useful expressions

probably / It's probable that …
possibly / It's possible that …
definitely / It's definitely (not) …
likely / It's likely that …
certainly / It's certain that …
It looks like / It looks as if …
I would say that …
It could be that …

4 **Speculate on the topics below with a partner. Give a reason for your view.**

Example: *I think the number of people who speak more than one language will probably decline in the future. Certainly, technology is going to make it easier to communicate in different languages.*

As you speak, your partner should complete the chart.

	topic	verb form	degree of certainty
a	the number of people who are bilingual	future 'will'	fairly certain
b	the use of translating machines		
c	the international spread of English		
d	an increase in world literacy		
e	the decline of the written word		
f	the importance of correct spelling and grammar		

Unit 16 *Mother tongue*

Understanding the writer's views

1 Read the texts below, taken from *The Cambridge Encyclopedia of Language*. Underline the key word[s] each paragraph and then complete the sentence be[s] each text, summarising the writer's main idea.

[Handwritten note:] HOMEWORK
Pg 106
answer questions
a, b, c, d, e

Pg 107
reading task

a It is difficult to know exactly how many languages exist today because ....
....
....

The [...] in the wo[...] [...]5,000, but est[...] [...]re is such un[...] [...]ose who wis[...] [...]ich preclude a simple answer to the question 'What counts as a language?'.

For most languages, the distinction between language and dialect is fairly clear-cut. In the case of English, for example, even though regional vocabulary and local differences of pronunciation can make communication difficult at times, no-one disputes the existence of an underlying linguistic unity that all speakers identify as English, and which is confirmed by the use of a standard written language.

b Although English is spoken in a number of ways, ...
....

c The dialects of China are ....
....
....

Because there has long been a single method for writing Chinese, and a common literary and cultural history, a tradition has grown up of referring to the eight main varieties of speech in China as 'dialects'. But, in fact, they are as different from each other (mainly in pronunciation and vocabulary) as French or Spanish is from Italian.

Language planning involves the creation and implementation of an official policy about how the languages and linguistic varieties of a country are to be used. Decisions of a fundamental nature may need to be made, especially in the developing countries. But planning issues are to be found in all countries, as people debate such topics as the place of minority languages, the role of an academy in safeguarding standards, the influence of the media on usage, and a host of other issues relating to education and standards in publishing.

d In both developing and developed nations, governments need to ....
....
....

e People have wondered for years about
....
....

For centuries, people have speculated over the origins of human language. What is the world's oldest language? Have all languages developed from a single source? How did words come to be, in the very beginning? These questions are fascinating, and have provoked experiments and discussion whose history dates back 3,000 years. The irony is that the search is a fruitless one.

Answers to Language Quiz
1 c) 2 a) 3 b) 4 a) 5 b) 6 c) 7 c) 8 a) 9 a) 10 b) (but nobody is sure!)

IELTS READING *YES / NO / NOT GIVEN*

*In the IELTS Reading test you may be asked to say whether a statement **agrees** with the view or claim of the writer, whether it **contradicts** the view or claim (i.e. it is the opposite) or whether the writer **says nothing about** this.*

To get going

Read the paragraph opposite and then look at the three statements below which illustrate the *Yes / No / Not given* question format.

a Saussure and his colleagues changed the way we investigate how people interact. ***YES** – this statement agrees with the writer's claims about Saussure.*

b Research into language follows the same methods as traditional scientific research. ***NO** – this statement does not agree with the writer's view. He makes a clear distinction between the methods used to study language and those used to study the physical world.*

c Humans are the only animals to have developed language. ***NOT GIVEN** – He says that language characterises humans but does not claim that humans are the only animals to have language.*

Key point: You will find something in the text that links to the topic of a NOT GIVEN question – here it is *animals* and *language* but the viewpoint related to this is not found in the passage.

Now follow Steps 1–3 below and do the IELTS Reading task which is based on the extracts on page 106.

> Born in Geneva in 1857, Ferdinand de Saussure is often referred to as the father of modern linguistics. With his contemporaries, Durkheim and Freud, <u>he helped to set the study of human behaviour on a new footing</u>. He recognised that we cannot study human beings and their institutions in the same way we might study a series of events in the physical world. For instance, a scientist can study the behaviour of objects under certain conditions, such as the reactions of a chemical substance to a variety of temperatures, <u>but human behaviour requires a different approach</u>. Saussure's treatment of language focuses on problems which are central to the relation between language and the human mind. <u>If we are to believe that man is indeed the 'language animal', a creature whose dealings with the world are characterised by human language, then it is Saussure who set us on this track.</u>

Step 1

Scan the short extracts on page 106 for words that might link the text with statement 1.

Step 2

Once you have found where the statement may come from, read that part of the text in detail and think about what it means. Re-phrase the material in your own words. Does it agree with the statement, contradict it, or say nothing about it? Decide whether the answer will be YES, NO or NOT GIVEN.

Step 3

Now do the same for the other statements 2–8.

IELTS READING TASK

Do the following statements agree with the views of the writer?

Write

YES	*if the statement agrees with the views of the writer*
NO	*if the statement contradicts the views of the writer*
NOT GIVEN	*if it is impossible to say what the writer thinks about this.*

1 There is little agreement on exactly how to define a language.
2 It is difficult to distinguish between a language and a dialect.
3 The fact that English has a standard written form makes it easy to learn.
4 It is inaccurate to describe the major varieties of Chinese as dialects.
5 Foreign languages should be taught in secondary schools.
6 Governments should avoid interfering in the way language is used.
7 Many people have tried to discover the origins of language.
8 Evidence shows that language dates back at least 3,000 years.

Academic and General Training Writing Task 2: For and against

In some IELTS Writing tasks you need to give arguments for and against the topic. If you do not do this you may only be answering half the question and you will lose marks.

✓ **Test tip**

You must keep the main topic in mind while you are writing and refer back to it all the time. You will lose marks if you do not address the issue raised in the question.

Re-writing or summarising the question

1 Read the Task 2 question below and summarise in your own words what it is that you must agree or disagree with.

> *Some governments try to control the way a national language is used. For example, they may restrict the introduction of foreign words, or the use of dialects, or they may demand that a certain language be used in schools.*
>
> *What are the benefits and disadvantages of these policies? Do you think they can ever be effective?*

2 Write your summary in the middle of a clean page and put a circle round it. 'Brainstorm' some ideas on how to respond to this question.

Making notes agreeing and disagreeing with the question

3 Organise your thoughts about the ideas in the task by writing them in your own words, and thinking of points for and against the argument.

Example:

Think of two more points to add to the notes, one *for* and one *against* the main topic in the circle.

FOR

Culture is maintained through language so it's worth keeping it pure.

One country needs one language.

Restrictions on a national language are justified.

AGAINST

Language is a living thing you can't stop it changing.

People have the right to use their own language.

Organising your answer

4 Now you need to make a plan for your answer. Here is an example.

Introduction
Expand the summary to re-phrase the question in your own words OR start with a clear statement of your own about the policy.

Paragraph 1
Expand the first point on the 'For' side about the link between language and culture. Balance it with a counter argument on the 'Against' side.

Paragraph 2
Express an opinion on having a national language. Give your own view. Make it clear to the reader where you stand or express an understanding of both points of view.

Paragraph 3
Include another point of your own based on your ideas above.

Conclusion
End with a clear statement on how you feel about the issue OR summarise the two main sides of the argument.

Useful expressions

The question of whether or not …
I feel that language is …

Some people think …
It can be argued that …
However, …

While …, there may be an argument in favour of …

I tend to think that …
Generally speaking, …

To sum up …
Ultimately, it is important to consider …

Writing a complete answer

5 Write a complete answer to this question, following the steps above.

> *Learning a foreign language offers an insight into how people from other cultures think and see the world. The teaching of a foreign language should be compulsory at all primary schools.*
>
> *To what extent do you agree or disagree with this view?*

✓ **Test tip**

'To what extent do you agree' is another way of saying 'Do you agree … If so, how much?' It invites you to agree and disagree.

IELTS *Test practice*

ACADEMIC READING Section 3

Questions 1 to 14 on page 111 are based on the reading passage below.

How does the human brain process language?
New studies into the use of sign language hint at an answer

One of the great mysteries of the human brain is how it understands and produces language. Until recently, most of the research on this subject had been based on the study of spoken languages: English, French, German and the like. Starting in the mid-19th century, scientists made large strides in identifying the regions of the brain involved in speech. For example, in 1861 the French neurologist Paul Broca discovered that patients who could understand spoken language but had difficulty speaking tended to have damage to a part of the brain's left hemisphere, later known as Broca's area. And in 1874 German physician Carl Wernicke found that patients with fluent speech but severe comprehension problems typically had damage to another part of the left hemisphere, which was then called Wernicke's area.

Similar damage to the brain's right hemisphere only very rarely results in such language disruptions, which are called 'aphasias'. Instead right hemisphere damage is more often associated with severe visual–spatial problems, such as the inability to copy a simple line drawing. For these reasons, the left hemisphere is often branded the verbal hemisphere and the right hemisphere the spatial hemisphere. Although this dichotomy[1] is an oversimplification, it does capture some of the main clinical differences between individuals with damage to the left side of the brain and those with damage to the right.

Nevertheless, many puzzles remain. One that has been particularly hard to crack is why language establishes itself in the brain where it does. The locations of Wernicke's and Broca's areas seem to make sense; Wernicke's area, involved in speech comprehension, is located near the part of the brain that receives signals from the ear. Broca's area, involved in speech production, is located next to the part of the brain that controls the muscles of the mouth and lips. But is the brain's organisation for language truly based on the functions of hearing and speaking? One way to explore this question is to study a language that uses different sensory and motor channels. Reading and writing, of course, employ vision for comprehension and hand movements for expression, but for most people these activities depend, at least in part, on brain systems involved in the use of a spoken language. The sign languages of the deaf, however, precisely fit the bill and are therefore perfect for such research.

Many people mistakenly believe that sign language is just a loose collection of pantomime-like gestures thrown together willy-nilly to allow rudimentary communication. But, in truth, sign languages are highly structured linguistic systems with all the

[1] division into two parts

grammatical complexity of spoken languages. Just as spoken languages have elaborate rules for forming words and sentences, sign languages have rules for individual signs and signed sentences. Contrary to another common misconception, there is no universal sign language. Deaf people in different countries use very different sign languages. In fact, a deaf signer[2] who acquires a second sign language as an adult will actually sign with a foreign accent! Moreover, sign languages are not simply manual versions of the spoken languages that are used in their surrounding communities. American Sign Language (ASL) and British Sign Language, for example, are mutually incomprehensible; in other words, users of these different languages cannot understand one another.

Spoken and sign languages share the abstract properties of language but differ radically in their outward form. Spoken languages involve the creation of vocal sounds made one after the other, while sign languages rely on visual–spatial changes, i.e. actions and movements, to signal linguistic contrasts. But there are also similarities. Sign languages, like spoken languages, have several kinds of linguistic structure, including phonological (sound), morphological (form) and syntactic (grammar) levels. Just as spoken words are composed of a small set of consonants and vowels, signs are made up of a small set of components which include hand shapes, the locations around the body where signs are made, the movements of the hands and arms and the orientation of the hands. So location of a sign is a critical element in conveying meaning. For example, palm up versus palm down. In American Sign Language the signs for the words 'summer', 'ugly' and 'dry' have the same hand shape, movement and orientation, but differ in location. 'Summer' is articulated near the forehead, 'ugly' near the nose and 'dry' near the chin.

At the morphological level, ASL has grammatical markers that systematically change the meaning of signs. In English these include fragments like 'ed' which can be added to most verbs to indicate past tense. However, in ASL the signs are modified using distinctive spatial patterns or types of movement. At the syntactical level, ASL specifies the grammatical relations among signs in ways that do not occur in spoken languages. In English, for instance, meaning is often embedded in word order. Take the example 'Mary criticised John'. Reverse the order of the names, and you reverse the meaning of the sentence. Signers of ASL can use word-order cues as well, but they need not. Instead they can point to a distinct position in space while signing a noun, thus linking the word with that position. Then the signer can move the verb sign from Mary's position to John's to mean 'John criticised Mary' and in the other direction to mean the reverse.

Over the past two decades, we have examined groups of deaf people who communicate through sign language, and who have suffered damage to either the right or the left hemisphere of their brains, mostly as a result of a stroke. By evaluating their proficiency at understanding and producing signs, we set out to determine whether the brain regions that interpret and generate sign language are the same ones involved in spoken language. The surprising results have illuminated the workings of the human brain and may help neurologists treat the ills of their deaf patients.

[2] someone who uses sign language

110

IELTS Test practice

Questions 1–6

Do the following statements reflect the claims of the writer in the reading passage?
Write

YES *if the statement agrees with the claims of the writer*
NO *if the statement contradicts the claims of the writer*
NOT GIVEN *if it is impossible to say what the writer thinks about this*

✓ Test tip

As the statements follow the order of information in the text, it is best to start with statement 1.

1 Initial research on how the brain processes language was carried out on European languages.
2 People who can speak but have trouble understanding language have damage to part of the left side of the brain.
3 The work of Broca was a great influence on that of Wernicke.
4 The right side of the brain is known as the verbal hemisphere.
5 Broca's area is concerned with understanding speech.
6 The first sign languages were created in the 19th century.

Questions 7–11

Write the correct letter A–C. Classify the following as referring to

A sign language only
B spoken language only
C both sign and spoken language

7 complex grammatical systems
8 influence of a person's first language on their second
9 small changes in form that change meaning
10 dependence on word order for meaning
11 the demonstration of a contrast through an action or movement

Questions 12–14

Choose THREE letters A–F.

*Which **THREE** issues are mentioned by the writer?*

12 **A** the relevance of aphasia to the study of sign language
B the relationship between the organisation of the brain and the functions of hearing and speaking
C the recent popularity of signing in America
D the difficulty of learning sign language
E the use of motion to create meaning in ASL
F the contribution of the research to the treatment of the deaf

Choose the correct letter, A, B, C or D.

13 Which word does this two-part sign diagram illustrate?
A summer
B ugly
C dry
D nose

14 The main purpose of the article is to
A clarify some facts about how the brain produces language.
B inform the reader about languages for the deaf.
C outline the basics of ASL.
D illustrate the research potential of sign language.

Answer key

UNIT 1 Take a break

SPEAKING PAGE 6

2–3
a	(go) skiing	e	(go) swimming
b	(go) shopping	f	(play) cards
c	(go) hiking	g	(go) (rock) climbing
d	(play) football/soccer	h	(go) (horse) riding

Play is used for games that involve team players or opponents; *go* is used for more individual activities that often take place away from home, i.e. you need to 'go' somewhere to do them.

4 Often there are no players and sometimes no movement is required. The emphasis is on the craft or skill. The activities are:
i cooking j singing k reading l sewing
m using the computer n drawing

5 *Possible answers*
I never go hiking, but I sometimes play football.
I really enjoy playing football.
I like playing cards. In fact, I usually play with friends every Friday evening.

LANGUAGE CHECK PAGE 7

1 a amazed b tiring

2 exhausting / exhausted boring / bored
relaxing / relaxed satisfying / satisfied
interesting / interested irritating / irritated
fascinating / fascinated revolting / revolted
a Professor Johnson is an interesting lecturer.
b This food is revolting.
c I'm fascinated by dinosaurs.
d I need a break. I'm exhausted.
e I'm afraid I'm not satisfied with this new phone.
f It's satisfying when you manage to find all the answers.
g Right now I'm watching TV. It's relaxing.

LISTENING PAGE 8

1 a photography b American football
c running d painting e surfing f chess
g table tennis h gardening

4–6
		conversation	clues	adjectives
a	Stamp collecting			
b	Running	6	marathon, distance, 26 miles	tired
c	Chess	2	the moves, keep his mind active	never bored
d	Tennis	1	court, opponent, match, sets	exhausted
e	Football			
f	Water polo	3	good swimmer, goal keeper	tough, exhausting
g	Gardening	5	grow, pots and window boxes, green fingers	satisfying
h	Fishing	4	river, catch anything	relaxing
i	Surfing			
j	Reading	7	novel, book	exciting

RECORDING SCRIPT CD 1 track 2

Conversation 1
Man: You look <u>exhausted</u>.
Woman: Yes, I've just come off the <u>court</u>.
Man: Did you win?
Woman: Yes … finally … but my <u>opponent</u> was very strong. The <u>match</u> went to three <u>sets</u>.
Man: Well done!

Conversation 2
Woman: When did you learn to play?
Man: When I was a child. My grandfather taught me the <u>moves</u> when I was only six years old. I <u>never get bored</u> – every game's a new <u>challenge</u>.
Woman: Really?
Man: Yes, we used to play every Sunday afternoon. He loved it.
Woman: It must have helped to <u>keep his mind active</u>.

Conversation 3
Woman 1: It looks like a really <u>tough</u> sport. I don't know how you do it.
Woman 2: Oh, I love it. But you've got to be a <u>good swimmer</u>.
Woman 1: I wouldn't want to be the <u>goal keeper</u>!
Woman 2: Yes, that's hard. We usually put our very best player in goal.
Woman 1: It looks <u>exhausting</u>!

Conversation 4
Woman: Don't you ever get bored?
Man: No, never. I just love sitting here by the <u>river</u>, doing nothing. It's so <u>relaxing</u>.

Woman: Do you ever <u>catch anything</u>?

Man: No, not often. But that doesn't matter.

Woman: It's not for me, I'm afraid. I need something a bit more interesting!

Conversation 5

Woman: People often think it's a hobby for old people. But I love it. It's very <u>satisfying</u> seeing things <u>grow</u>.

Man: Yes, but we live in an apartment.

Woman: You can grow things in <u>pots and window boxes</u>, you know. You don't need a lot of space.

Man: Perhaps I should give it a try.

Woman: Yes, you might find you have <u>green fingers</u> after all!

Conversation 6

Woman: Would you like to join us for dinner on Saturday?

Man: Thanks, but I can't. I need to be ready for the <u>marathon</u> on Sunday.

Woman: Oh, OK. What <u>distance</u> do you have to cover?

Man: <u>26 miles</u>, so I'll need to be in bed early.

Woman: 26 miles! That makes me feel <u>tired</u> just thinking about it!

Conversation 7

Woman: Are you enjoying the latest Harry Potter <u>novel</u>?

Man: Oh, it's great! It's really <u>exciting</u>. I can't put it down.

Woman: I thought the film was better, myself.

Man: I haven't seen the film yet.

Woman: Actually, I usually find I prefer the <u>book</u> to the film, but not this time.

7 a collecting model cars OR painting OR drawing
  b (microlight) flying / flying small/light (aero)planes
  c 14 d (the) excitement e a bird

RECORDING SCRIPT CD 1 track 3

Interviewer: Good morning! Today on *Hobby Horse* we'll be hearing about some unusual hobbies. Maybe you had a hobby when you were a child, such as <u>collecting model cars</u>, or <u>painting or drawing</u>. But not many of us continue with these hobbies into our adult life. John Shipley is an exception, however. He's on the line to tell us about his rather unusual hobby that has taken him to high places.

John Shipley: Hello.

Interviewer: Tell us, when did you first become interested in planes?

John Shipley: When I was about seven years old. I've always loved the idea of flying.

Interviewer: And what kind of planes do you fly?

John Shipley: <u>Very light planes, called microlights</u>.

Interviewer: What age must you be before you can take up flying a microlight?

John Shipley: You must be at least <u>14</u> to have lessons. You do this with an instructor but you can't 'go solo' – that's flying on your own, until you are 15.

Interviewer: What is it that you like so much about this leisure activity? It sounds like it could be quite dangerous.

John Shipley: Oh ... lots of things. The sense of freedom – being able to get away from everything, but I think, <u>most of all, it's the excitement</u>.

Interviewer: Yes, it must be fantastic being up in the air like that.

John Shipley: It's <u>like being a bird</u>. There's nothing else like it!

Step up to IELTS SPEAKING PAGE 9

The Speaking test model was recorded by one of the authors and a native speaker to illustrate the format and content of Part 1. For the recording script please go to www.cambridge.org/elt/stepup

READING PAGE 10

1 scan: a, b, d
  skim: c, e

2 a To inform readers about a new book.
    To advertise the sale of some cheap socks.
    To advertise an art auction.
  b Magazine or newspaper readers, students
    Newspaper reader, general public.
    Art dealers, newspaper readers
  c Saturn / spacecraft / prepare yourself / book
    Sale / $ / City Superstore / the general layout
    Modern and contemporary / Auction / On View / the general layout

3 a Cassini b July 2004 c $4.99 (for two pairs)
  d Monday 2 December

WRITING PAGE 11

1 b ✗ To ask formal permission
  c ✔ To thank someone for something
  d ✗ To provide information
  e ✔ To give an official apology
  f ✗ To make an official complaint

2 *Possible answers*
  a Dear (Rosemary); Lots of love
  b Dear Dr/ Professor ...; Yours sincerely
  c Dear (Mr and) Mrs / Dear Rosemary; Kind regards / Best wishes
  d Dear Sir; Yours faithfully
  e Dear Mr/Mrs ...; Kind regards / Best wishes
  f Dear Sir/Sirs; Yours faithfully

3 a v b i c ii d iv e iii

4 i 10 ii 4 iii 8 iv 11 v 5, 9, 10

IELTS TEST PRACTICE PAGES 12–13

1 aerobics 2 twice a week
3 Olympic coaches 4 (on) public holidays
5 Any level / beginners to advanced
6 School programmes
7 at/from the centre / at/from The Edge
8 E 9 D 10 F 11 C 12 A 13 B

UNIT 2 What's on the menu?

Step up to **IELTS READING** PAGES 14–15

2 a Norway/Australia b Queen Elizabeth II
   c bees d McDonald's e apple, lemon

IELTS task

1 1902 2 45 kilograms 3 white 4 frostbite
5 fibre, vitamins, minerals
6 C 7 B 8 G 9 F 10 E 11 A
12 A + H 13 D + F 14 E + G

SPEAKING PAGES 16–17

RECORDING SCRIPT CD1 tracks 5, 6, 7

Exercise 2

Speaker 1: I don't like vegetables and I really hate cabbage.
Speaker 2: I'm afraid I can't stand cream or anything that's made with it.
Speaker 3: Don't you think cold coffee's really horrible?

Exercise 3

Speaker 1: I love eating vegetables, especially cabbage.
Speaker 2: I really like cream and anything that's made with it.
Speaker 3: I adore iced coffee – it's delicious.

Exercise 4

Speaker 1: I'm afraid I just don't eat meat.
Speaker 2: I just don't eat cheese at all.
Speaker 3: I can't stand the smell of fish.
Speaker 1: I just love the taste of ice cream.
Speaker 2: I hate what toffee does to my teeth.
Speaker 3: I just really like sweet things.

5 *taste/flavour:* bitter, bland, fatty, fizzy, greasy, hot, juicy, salty, sour, spicy, sweet
texture: chewy, creamy, crunchy, fatty, juicy, stodgy, tough
smell/aroma: bitter, sickly, sweet
the effect food has on us: fattening, filling, refreshing

6 a fattening b greasy c refreshing
   d spicy/hot e filling f fizzy g bitter h salty

LISTENING PAGE 18

2

		conversation	clues
a	Take-away restaurant	4	menu /15-minute wait / come back / collect
b	Own kitchen	7	bought / go and get / guests / finish this dessert
c	Friend's house	3	curry / recipe / her kitchen
d	Outdoor barbecue	5	sausages / steaks / kebabs / 12 people / fire / cook
e	College canteen	2	queue / tray / their table
f	Plane	6	wrapped in plastic / travelling
g	Restaurant	1	order / chefs

RECORDING SCRIPT CD1 track 8

Conversation 1

Waitress: Are you ready to order, sir?
Customer: Yes. I'd like the steak, but can I have salad instead of chips?
Waitress: Of course. Anything to drink?
Customer: Just water, please.
Waitress: Fine. It'll be about fifteen minutes, I'm afraid. One of our chefs is off sick.
Customer: Oh, don't worry.

Conversation 2

Student 1: I'm starving. I think I'll get in the queue for the hot food today.
Student 2: I'll just have a sandwich. I'll be cooking tonight.
Student 1: Here's a tray.
Student 2: Thanks. Shall we go and sit with Bob and Tina at their table?
Student 1: OK. It's pretty busy in here today.

Conversation 3

Man: Mmm. This curry's delicious, isn't it?
Woman: Yes, and the onion dish really adds to the flavour.
Man: Let's ask Mary for the recipe when she comes out of her kitchen.
Woman: Good idea!

Conversation 4

Customer: Have you got a menu?
Waiter: Yes, here you are. Sweet and sour pork is off.
Customer: OK. We'll have fried prawns, beef in chilli sauce and steamed rice.
Waiter: There's a 15-minute wait.
Customer: OK. We'll come back later to collect it.

Conversation 5

Man: Now, I've got sausages, steaks and kebabs … anything else?
Woman: That's it. Do you think it's enough for 12 people?
Man: Oh sure. There's plenty of salad to go with it.
Woman: Is the fire hot enough yet?
Man: I think so. What shall we cook first?

Conversation 6

Child: I don't feel very hungry at the moment.
Parent: Never mind. Eat what you can.
Child: It would taste much better if it wasn't wrapped in plastic.
Parent: Just pretend you're at home.
Child: I wish I was. I hate travelling.

Conversation 7

Husband: Now where did I put the lemons that I bought yesterday?
Wife: Here they are, Nick.
Husband: Thanks. Oh dear, they aren't very juicy.
Wife: Do you want me to go and get some more?
Husband: Yes, please. Our guests will be here in half an hour and I need to finish this dessert.

3 a last night / the previous night/evening
   b aunt and cousin c a Japanese restaurant
   d chicken e sashimi f tea

RECORDING SCRIPT CD1 track 9

Woman: ... I went out for dinner <u>last night</u>. 'Cos <u>my aunt and my cousin</u> had come to see me for the evening so I decided to take them out. I was going to take them to my favourite Italian café ... yes, the Napoli ... but it was fully booked so we <u>ended up eating at the new Japanese restaurant</u> near the city centre ... Yes, that's the one! It was really nice inside and they had several set menus at a variety of prices. ... Yes, well the one we chose was very good value for money. ... Well, my aunt ordered soup ... and <u>Martin, my cousin, had chicken</u>. Yes ... and I chose the <u>sashimi</u> – you know, raw fish. <u>I'd never eaten that before</u> but I quite liked it. It has a very delicate flavour. My cousin had beer but my aunt and <u>I had tea</u>.

4 a The simple past tense, because the event took place 'last night'.
  b The Italian café.
  c The past continuous tense is used because the speaker is describing a plan that had to be changed.
  d The simple past.

5 I *was going to take* them to my favorite Italian café ... yes, the Napoli ... but it was fully booked so we *ended up eating* at the new Japanese restaurant.

6 *Possible answer*
  I was going to study Biology but I ended up studying French instead.

IELTS TEST PRACTICE PAGES 19–21

1 chemistry
2 *any two of:* flavours / ingredients / processing methods
3 *any two of:* flavours / ingredients / processing methods
4 B   5 D   6 B   7 C   8 A
9 cheese, coffee, tea   10 smell / aroma(s)
11 quality control (purposes)
12 (an) electronic tongue   13 vanilla extract

UNIT 3 *On the road*

LISTENING PAGE 22

2 a handle   b name tag   c strap   d wheels
3 Suitcase: b, g, i, j, k, l   bag: f, h
  rucksack: c, e   briefcase: d   case: a
4 a It's a small plastic case with a handle and a shoulder strap.
  b It's a suitcase made of fabric with a zip.
  c It's a small rucksack with a pocket on the front.
  d It's a thin plastic briefcase.
  e It's a rucksack with a pocket on the side and a sleeping bag on top.
  f It's a canvas bag with a zip fastening, a shoulder strap, and a name tag.
  g It's a set of three suitcases.
  h It's a bag with a zip, handles on top and a pocket with a buckle on the side.
  i It's an old suitcase with a name tag and lots of stickers.
  j It's a suitcase with two straps.
  k It's a plastic suticase on wheels.
  l It's a suitcase on wheels and it has a strap with a big buckle.

6

conversation	bag	key words
1	e	yellow, pocket, sleeping bag
2	g	coming together, small one, other two
3	d	green briefcase
4	f	black, not brown
5	i	dirty old suitcase, stickers
6	j	large, red suitcase, yellow straps

RECORDING SCRIPT CD1 track 10

Conversation 1
Woman: What kind of bag have you got?
Man: It's a rucksack.
Woman: Is it that small, pink rucksack over there?
Man: No, mine's <u>yellow with a front pocket</u>. And it should have my <u>sleeping bag</u> tied on to the top. I hope they haven't lost it. Oh good! There it is!

Conversation 2
Child: Mum! Mum! I can see our cases coming now.
Mother: Can you? Where are they?
Child: Over there! Look! They're all <u>coming through together</u>.
Mother: You get <u>the small one</u> and I'll grab the other two.

Conversation 3
Woman: I can't believe it takes this long to get the bags off the plane.
Man: Just be patient, dear. They'll arrive in a minute. Ah! There's my <u>green briefcase</u>.
Woman: But ... no sign of my bags.
Man: No. Isn't that your brown suitcase coming through now?
Woman: No. I can't see it anywhere.

Answer key

Conversation 4

Father: There's your bag, Chris. Can you grab it?
Boy: No, Dad. That's not our bag. Ours is <u>black, not brown</u>. And it's bigger than that.
Father: Oh, you're right. They all look so similar, don't they?
Boy: Ah, I can see it. It's coming now.

Conversation 5

Man 1: Oh, at last! They've started loading the bags from our flight. Here they come.
Man 2: Look at that <u>dirty, old suitcase</u> with all the <u>stickers</u> on it! That person has done some travelling.
Man 1: Yeah! That's my bag actually.
Man 2: Oh, really?

Conversation 6

Woman: Excuse me – would you mind grabbing my suitcase for me?
Man: Sure – what does it look like?
Woman: It's that one there – the <u>large, red suitcase with the two yellow straps</u> round the outside.
Man: There you are!
Woman: Thanks so much.
Man: Not a problem.

Step up to IELTS LISTENING PAGE 23

1 International (Hotel) 2 0793 665 091
3 QF2 4 London / UK 5 31(st) (of) July
6 small 7 handle on top 8 brown 9 leather
10 with wheels / on wheels

RECORDING SCRIPT CD1 tracks 11 & 12

Questions 1–5

Man: Yes, can I help you?
Woman: Two of my bags seem to be missing.
Man: Where were you coming from, madam?
Woman: From London via Bangkok.
Man: OK – I'll have to get you to fill out this form.
Woman: I'm sorry. I don't have my glasses with me. Would you mind reading it to me?
Man: Right. Can I have your name please, madam?
Woman: Greenleaf – Mrs <u>Mary Greenleaf</u> – that's G-R-E-E-N-L-E-A-F.
Man: Address?
Woman: Here, or in the UK? We live in Manchester.
Man: Here in Sydney. Where are you staying?
Woman: <u>We're staying at the International Hotel.</u>
Man: And the phone number there?
Woman: I'll give you my husband's mobile number. It's 0793 …
Man: <u>0793 …</u>
Woman: <u>665 091.</u>
Man: 655 091.
Woman: No – 665 091.
Man: Right. And which flight were you on?
Woman: Flight <u>QF2</u>.
Man: That's the flight from Bangkok, isn't it?
Woman: Well, we stopped briefly in Bangkok, but <u>the bags were loaded in the UK. We've come through from London.</u>
Man: And what date did you board the flight?
Woman: We left London yesterday – that was the <u>31st of July</u>.
Man: OK … departed 31st July. Two bags, you said?
Woman: Yes, that's right.

Questions 6–10

Man: Now – what sort of bags are we looking for?
Woman: Well – there's one that has all my make-up in it and …
Man: Can you give me a thorough description of it, madam?
Woman: Yes, <u>it's a small, square case, made of blue plastic</u>.
Man: And does it have your name on it anywhere?
Woman: Not anywhere visible. I think my name is written inside.
Man: Right … and does it have a handle of any sort?
Woman: Yes, it's got a <u>handle on top</u>.
Man: That's useful; it'll help us find it. … OK. And the other one?
Woman: Well – that's a suitcase. It's a medium sized, <u>brown, leather</u> suitcase.
Man: <u>Brown leather</u>, you said?
Woman: Yes.
Man: Does it have a strap round it or anything?
Woman: No … but <u>it's got its own wheels</u>.
Man: Suitcase … <u>with wheels</u>.
Woman: You know, his has never happened to me before. I hope they turn up.
Man: Oh, they always turn up, madam. Chances are they'll be on the next flight in from Bangkok.

READING PAGE 24

1 The Mekong flows through China, Myanmar (Burma), Thailand, Laos, Cambodia and Vietnam.

2 a In a magazine or newspaper or travel magazine.
  b To encourage people to visit the area. To entertain.
  c Tourists or travellers.
  d He likes it very much. (A model town … the perfect market … in this amazing land)

3 car, ferry, walking, bicycle, speedboat

Step up to IELTS READING PAGE 25

1 6/six 2 Ho Chi Minh 3 car
4 on foot 5 teachers/schools 6 schoolchildren/schoolgirls/students 7 Sam Mountain
8 spectacular 9 speed

WRITING PAGE 26

Sample answer
The diagram illustrates how an electronic tracking device can be fitted to someone's clothing or hidden in a bag, in order to allow that person to be tracked and located. There are three basic stages to the process.
(38 words)

3 1 bag or on the person's clothing 2 is monitored
  3 is sent / is transmitted 4 a transmission tower
  5 re-transmitted 6 mobile phone
  7 a computer / an internet website 8 street
  9 map / screen

116

Sample paragraph 4

A device of this nature could be very effective as a means of tracking and locating someone such as a school child.

IELTS TEST PRACTICE PAGE 27

1 $14   2 (has) swimming pool   3 (scuba) diving
4 $30   5 (own) bathroom   6 fishing   7 Shute
Harbour 8 Golden Sands   9 $4 an hour /
$4 per hour / $4/hour   10 soap and toothpaste

RECORDING SCRIPT CD1 track 13

Questions 1–6

Woman: Good morning, East Coast Backpackers.

Traveller: Oh, hi. I'd like some information, please.

Woman: Yes, sure.

Traveller: How much does it cost to stay at your hostel?

Woman: Well – if you stay in the bunkhouse, it's $5.90 a night – that's sharing with five other people.

Traveller: Right – do you have anything else? We didn't really want to share with that many people.

Woman: Sure! We've got cabins for $11 a night or, if you want air conditioning, then they're $14.

Traveller: So … the cabins with air conditioning are $14?

Woman: Correct.

Traveller: OK. Are you right on the beach?

Woman: It's a five-minute walk to the beach, and we also have a swimming pool.

Traveller: What about diving? Can you do any scuba diving?

Woman: Sure. And we offer a special package for diving.

Traveller: Great. I'll get back to you.

Man: Hello, Emu Park Hostel.

Traveller: Oh, hi. I'm just inquiring about the cost of staying at your hostel.

Man: Well … we've got a number of levels of accommodation. If you share with up to five others, it'll cost you $5 a night or $30 a week.

Traveller: Do you have any individual rooms?

Man: Yeah, we do. We've got rooms overlooking the beach … with their own bathroom.

Traveller: How much are the rooms with the bathroom?

Man: $30 a night, but we're booked out for the rest of the month.

Traveller: Oh, I see. And is it possible to scuba dive? I mean, are there any diving facilities?

Man: Not here, I'm afraid. But it's great for fishing.

Traveller: OK. Not too keen on fishing, thanks. I might leave it, then.

Questions 7–10

Woman: Hello, East Coast Backpackers.

Traveller: Oh, hi. It's Sabine Thoma here again. I called you earlier.

Woman: Oh, yes. I remember.

Traveller: I'd like to make a reservation, if that's possible, for the bunkhouse.

Woman: Fine. What dates were you looking at?

Traveller: Well … from today, if possible for about a week.

Woman: Oh! OK … well you're in luck because some people have just left this morning.

Traveller: Can you give me the exact address, please?

Woman: OK, well, it's the Backpackers' Hostel, Shute Harbour Road – that's S-H-U-T-E and another word, 'harbour', which is spelt H-A-R-B-O-U-R.

Traveller: Shute Harbour Road, … OK, got it. And how do we get there from the town? We'll be arriving by coach.

Woman: Well, you'll need to take a local bus. Catch the number 25 to the beach. It will have the words 'Golden Sands' on the front of the bus.

Traveller: Right – let me just write that down … Golden Sands.

Woman: Just ask for the Backpackers' Hostel. But it's only two kilometres from the centre of town, so you could walk it.

Traveller: I think we'll get the bus. Oh, and one last thing. Do you have access to the internet?

Woman: Yes. We've got a little internet café here, with five computers. So you can send and receive emails.

Traveller: And how much does it cost to use the computers?

Woman: That'll cost you $4 an hour. And we serve great coffee too!

Traveller: So … is there a little shop where we can buy things?

Woman: Yes, we sell a few essential things, you know, soap and toothpaste, that sort of thing.

Traveller: Thanks. That sounds perfect. We'll see you this evening.

Woman: Right, Sabine, we'll see you then.

UNIT 4 All at sea

SPEAKING PAGE 28

3

beach	shipping	marine life
currents	boat	dolphin
lifeguard	captain	octopus
rocks	cargo	organisms
salt	lighthouse	plankton
sand	oceans	seaweed
shell	sailor	shark
shore	ship	
tide		
wave		

READING PAGE 29

2 b

3 *Possible answer:* The seabed

4 Para B Main idea: How the seas were formed (*this would also be a possible heading*)
Para C Main idea: The first sea life (*this would also be a possible heading*)
Para B *Possible heading:* Chemical content of the sea
Para C *Possible heading:* Origins of marine life

Possible title: The sea / Origins of the sea

6 a peak
  b creatures
  c immense numbers / vast numbers
  d minute /maɪˈnjuːt/
  e surface
  f fossil
  g marine
  h continents

Step up to IELTS READING PAGE 30

2 ships and cargoes

3 satellite navigation technology

4 Spain

5 Christopher Columbus' uncle / Antonio Columbus

6 a sandy seabed / sand

7 computerised (marine) charts

LANGUAGE CHECK PAGE 31

1 Paragraph A: more varied, the highest, the deepest, the biggest
Paragraph B: rarer, saltier
Paragraph C: the biggest, the smallest, bigger

2 a the most significant
  b more convenient; less personal
  c quicker
  d the spiciest
  e better; better

4 a Whereas
  b On the other hand
  c While
  d whereas
  e On the other hand
  f Whereas
  g whereas
  h While

WRITING PAGE 32

1 a for washing clothes   b for their gardens

2 a A pie chart is an analogue chart. The segments are percentages of the whole, i.e. together they represent 100%. In a bar chart, the values are given along one axis, and each bar represents what is being compared or measured along the other axis. They do not *necessarily* add up to 100%.
  b Both charts describe water usage but in different situations. B is a subsidiary of A.
  c The different ways in which water is used in households/homes.
  d A, because it includes the information in B.
  e The fact that irrigation uses the most water and the disproportionate amount of household water used in gardens and swimming pools. (Other answers are possible.)

3 a water usage/consumption
  b household water usage/consumption
  c higher/larger   d irrigation   e industry

4 *Sample answer*
From Chart B we can see that by far the largest proportion of domestic water, well over 50% in fact, goes into gardens and swimming pools. Drinking and cooking account for a smaller volume of water consumption than personal hygiene and clothes washing, which together make up about 25%.
A very small percentage of water is used for other purposes which are not identified in the chart. When read together, the two charts provide a useful overview of water use in Australia.

5 The diagram is a cross section of the sea shore, showing the different zones made by high and low tides.

6 a cross section / profile   b low and high
  c intertidal zone   d under water / submerged
  e sand dunes

IELTS TEST PRACTICE PAGE 33

Sample answer
(First paragraph explains what the diagrams show and describes the first diagram).

The two diagrams illustrate the shape and formation of the land under the sea. The first profile provides a cross section of the coast of a continent beneath the surface of the sea, and illustrates that the continental shelf goes to a depth of approximately 200 metres below sea level. The land then drops abruptly to the bottom of the ocean, which is known as the sea floor.

(Second paragraph describes second diagram).

The second diagram focuses on the depth of the ocean and the amount of light that penetrates to the bottom. Sea level is shown as 0 m and the first 200 m below the surface is referred to as the sunlight zone. This is where the continental shelf ends. Below this is the twilight zone, which descends for 800 m. The water temperature shown is approximately 5 °C in this zone. The area between 1000 m and 4000 m is known as the dark zone, with a water temperature of 1–2 °C. Almost no light can penetrate this far down.

(160 words)

UNIT **5** *Come rain or shine*

LISTENING PAGE 34

2, 3

1	c	✔	safe and secure
2	a	✘	traffic worse in rain
3	d	✔	rain badly needed
4	b	✘	get soaked / wet clothes

RECORDING SCRIPT CD1 tracks 15 and 16

Exercises 2 and 3

Presenter: And welcome to today's phone-in! So let's go to our first caller who is .... Jane. Good morning, Jane.
Jane: Good morning.
Presenter: Now we've been having our fair share of rain this month. How do you feel about this wet weather?
Jane: Oh. It's great! I love the rain.
Presenter: Oh really? Why's that, Jane?
Jane: Well, I just love the sound of it on the window. Especially when I'm tucked up in bed ... it makes me feel safe and secure.
Presenter: And do you have a musical request this morning?
Jane: Yes. I'd like to hear *Stormy Monday Blues*.
Presenter: OK, Jane. *Stormy Monday Blues* coming up.

Presenter: And our next caller is Bruno. Are you there, Bruno?
Bruno: Hi.
Presenter: Bruno – where are you calling from?
Bruno: Melbourne.
Presenter: The line's not very clear, mate!
Bruno: That's 'cos I'm calling on my mobile and I'm stuck in the traffic.
Presenter: What do you think of this weather we've been having?
Bruno: Oh! It's terrible. It's driving me mad! The traffic's always worse when it rains.
Presenter: Well, we need it, you know!
Bruno: Yeah, but not this much.
Presenter: OK ... so what would you like to hear this morning?

Presenter: So, Bruno didn't think much of this weather. Let's take another call. Mary!
Mary: Hello ... can you hear me!
Presenter: Yes, we can hear you. Where are you calling from, Mary?
Mary: From a property in the far west of Victoria. We're on a sheep farm here.
Presenter: And what do you think of this rain?
Mary: Oh ... It's marvellous! It's been dry as a bone here for months. We desperately needed the rain. We haven't seen decent rain for over two years.
Presenter: Yes – it's terrible for the farmers when there's a long drought. But that's a familiar pattern in the bush. Too much rain or not enough! Let's play a little song about the rain.

Presenter: Let's take another call. And this time it's Liz from the suburb of Carlton in Melbourne.
Liz: Hello!
Presenter: Are you enjoying all this rain we're having in Melbourne?
Liz: No ... I can't stand it. I much prefer the sunshine.
Presenter: Why's that, Liz? It's good for the garden.
Liz: Yes, but when it rains this much, you get soaked going to school and then you have to spend the whole day sitting around in wet clothes.
Presenter: Have you thought of taking an umbrella or a rain coat?
Liz: Oh, no. I couldn't use an umbrella. You look so stupid carrying an umbrella. No, I'd rather get wet.
Presenter: OK, Liz. And what would you like us to play for you today?

Exercise 4

Presenter: OK, so let's go to our first caller. Hello! And what's your name?
And where are you calling from? ...
And what's the weather like there today? ...
Is it? And do you like that kind of weather? ...
OK. And what would you like us to play for you today? ...

6 a shade
b the sun / the heat
c the (ancient) Greeks
d Italy
e position in society
f steel frame
g two (people)

RECORDING SCRIPT CD1 track 17

Presenter: Well, with all this rain about, we thought we'd do a bit of research into the origin of umbrellas. Where did umbrellas come from and why were they introduced? Let's go over to our resident specialist, Kerry McCall. What have you got for us on umbrellas, Kerry?

Kerry: Quite a bit, actually, John. Well … the English word 'umbrella' comes from the Latin word 'umbra' which <u>means 'shade'</u>. This is because the original umbrellas weren't used to protect you from the rain, but they were used to protect you <u>from the sun</u> in hot climates such as India, Egypt and China. Carrying an umbrella was seen as a sign that you were an important person. Ordinary people were expected to bake in the sun!

Umbrellas were introduced into Europe <u>by the ancient Greeks</u> to keep them cool, but it was the Romans who first thought to use them to keep themselves dry! Perhaps there wasn't very much rain in ancient Greece! Not like here, eh? There isn't much information available on umbrellas throughout the Middle Ages, <u>but by the late 1500s we see umbrellas being used again in Italy</u>. As in earlier days, we find the important people using umbrellas because having an umbrella reflected your … <u>your position in society</u>. But by the 1600s umbrellas were common in France and a century later they were everywhere in Europe. In 1850, the traditional umbrellas, which were made out of cane, were replaced with umbrellas with a steel frame. Because they were stronger, this meant that they could also be much bigger, and we see the first of the really large 'man-size' umbrellas, big enough <u>for two people</u>.

In modern English, the word 'umbrella' usually indicates something you would use to keep yourself *dry* rather than cool, but we do also talk about a 'beach umbrella', which is obviously not to protect you from the rain …

WRITING PAGES 36–37

1 a They provide information about the annual temperatures and rainfall in two Australian cities: Brisbane and Melbourne.
b The tables are exactly the same in layout and contain parallel information.
c They do not provide percentages. They provide raw data.

2 *Possible answers*
Melbourne has a cooler, slightly drier climate than Brisbane.
January is a warmer month in Brisbane than in Melbourne.
Melbourne has a colder climate than Brisbane.
The months of April and July are colder in Melbourne than in Brisbane.

3 a In Melbourne, the hottest month is January.
b The coolest time of year in Melbourne is in July.
c July is the coolest time of year in Brisbane.
d The wettest period in Brisbane is in January.
e The driest period in Melbourne is in January.
f Melbourne has the least number of rainy days in January.
g Brisbane has the most rainy days in January and the least rainy days in July.

4 *Possible answers*
a In Melbourne, the hottest month is January, when the average temperature goes as high as 26 °C during the day.
b The coolest time of year in Melbourne is in July. At this time of year, temperatures drop to as low as 4 °C.
c July is the coolest time of year in Brisbane, but even then the minimum average temperature does not go below 11 °C.
d The wettest period in Brisbane is in January, when they receive 169 mm of rain.
e The driest period in Melbourne is in January, although the rainfall in that month is only 1 mm less than in July.
f Melbourne has the least number of rainy days in January – only 8 days.
g Brisbane has the most rainy days in January and the least rainy days in July; that is 14 days and 7 days respectively.

6 *Possible answers*
a There are more rainy days in July in Melbourne than in Brisbane. However, in January Brisbane is the wetter of the two cities.
b October is the wettest month in Melbourne, whereas January is the wettest month in Brisbane. They both have an average of 14 rainy days at these times.
c July is the coldest month in both Brisbane and Melbourne, but/however the maximum temperatures in Brisbane are considerably higher than in Melbourne.
d In January, the amount of rain that falls in Brisbane is much greater than in Melbourne although Brisbane has only six more days of rain.
e There is a difference of only 8°C between the maximum and minimum temperatures in Brisbane in summer, whereas in Melbourne the difference is larger. On the other hand this difference decreases in winter in July.

7 a warmer
b temperature
c 11°C
d colder

8 *Sample answer*

Both Melbourne and Brisbane have a good annual rainfall. Brisbane, however, receives almost twice as much rain as Melbourne, while it has fewer wet days. The wettest months in both cities are January and October, although neither city has a totally dry season, according to the data.

Step up to IELTS GENERAL TRAINING WRITING PAGE 38

Possible answers

a storm/flood/hurricane
b the roof/house
c frightening/annoying/distressing
d loss/anger/fear
e damaged / flooded / burnt down
f repairs
g renovate the house / improve it
h in the holidays / can come and paint
i drop me a line / give me a ring

Sample answer

Dear Anna and Leo,

We were shocked to hear from Lara about the storm that hit your city recently and the damage done to your house. How awful to come home from your holiday to find the roof blown off the house!

I understand how you must feel, as we had a similar experience a few years ago when there was a sudden electrical storm here in Sydney. I came home from work to find that a tree had fallen on top of the house and all the windows were broken. Fortunately the insurance covered the cost of the repairs, but it was still very upsetting.

I suppose you have to think positively in situations like this and look at the opportunity you have to improve your house – give it a new look. If we can do anything for you in the holidays, we'd be happy to help.

Drop us a line and let us know.

Best wishes,   (*152 words*)

IELTS TEST PRACTICE PAGE 39

Sample answer

Dear Sir,

I have just returned home after spending three nights at your hotel in Paddington. The staff were very friendly and the location is extremely convenient. However, I feel I must express my disappointment about the room.

As we all know, London is experiencing a very warm summer this year, with temperatures around 30 °C last week, which is quite unusual. As a result, it was very hot in my room on the sixth floor.

Because of the extreme heat in the room, I had to leave the windows open all night and so it was very noisy, as the hotel is on a main road and the traffic never stops in London. Consequently, I got very little sleep over the three days.

I think it would be a good idea to install an air-conditioning system in the hotel. This could also be used as a heating system in the winter and would certainly make the rooms more comfortable. Perhaps you would consider giving me a discount if I come to your hotel again.

I look forward to hearing from you.

Yours faithfully,   (*185 words*)

UNIT 6 Value for money

READING PAGE 40

a value b currency c exchange d change
e inflation f trade g account
h paper money i bill j banknotes k prices

Step up to IELTS READING PAGE 41

1 *two of the following:* shells, butter, salt

2	(the) Chinese	8	12 / twelve
3	Kublai Khan	9	gold, silver
4	Sweden	10	printer
5	Bank of England	11	smaller countries
6	(the) euro	12	Australia
7	14 billion	13	Hong Kong

LISTENING PAGE 42

1 1 c 2 h 3 g 4 b/d 5 e/f 6 a 7 e/f
3 1 a 2 c 3 a

RECORDING SCRIPT CD 1 track 18

Speaker 1: You may think that people's spending doesn't change very much over the year but, as you can see from this graph, it does vary. There are two distinct periods when we spend more and that's <u>in the second and fourth quarters of the year ... you see these two peaks.</u> Otherwise the pattern is fairly stable.

Speaker 2: There are always fluctuations in our staff absentee rate. It's often affected by viruses that go round the office ... coughs and colds, that sort of thing. They result in periods when a lot of staff may be off at the same time. Over the first four months of this year, for example, the figures show that considerably <u>more staff were off sick in January</u> – that's a bad time for illness – but <u>then numbers gradually declined and in April we had almost no-one absent from work.</u>

Speaker 3: And what about trade? As you can see from this graph, our data shows that between 1997 and 2000 <u>China's international trade levels rose dramatically in comparison with global trade</u>, which showed steady but less significant growth.

4 1 US/Canada – b   2 Europe – a
  3 South America – e   4 Pacific Rim – d
  5 India – c

RECORDING SCRIPT CD1 track 19

Sales director: So, let's have a look at how the company has done over the year. This graph compares sales for most of our holiday destinations.

As you can see, sales of cruise holidays to Canada and the US did moderately well. They fluctuated throughout most of the year, then there was a slight dip towards the end of the year. However, this sector ended the year at an all-time high.

After a disappointing start, interest in our European package holidays increased in February and continued this trend, peaking in May. After that, there was a slight fall, after which sales stabilised for some time. Unfortunately, the last two months of the year saw a dramatic drop in sales.

Now, our biggest growth area last year was South America. Sales of holidays to places like Brazil and Argentina rose rapidly in the first half of the year and even though they levelled off mid-year, the sector remained stable until the end of the year.

For some reason, the number of long-haul flights to Pacific Rim destinations plummeted at the start of the year. Then, things hit a fairly low plateau until August, at which time they underwent a steep rise, ending the year at quite a high point.

Lastly, India was a popular tourist destination and flight sales rose in the first few months of the year. However, this situation didn't last and sales fell rather dramatically after that. This trend stabilised towards the end of the year, however, and there are signs that it will improve next year.

WRITING PAGE 43

1 spend, has risen, spent, spent, is expected, will rise
2 *Possible answers*
  a are predicted to rise
  b will take up / give up
  c is expected to fall
  d Tour operators predict that
3 a PS b PP c PP d PS e PS f F g PP
  h F i PS j F k F l PP
4 *Possible answers*

a	show / indicate	f	have changed
b	is predicted	g	predicted
c	to fall	h	will come
d	came from	i	is likely
e	were produced	j	is expected

Sample answer 1
Note: *This answer is less than 150 words because this first Step-up task is not a full exam question.*

(The opening paragraph states what the graph shows and describes the main trend.)

The graph is about the number of people in China who own vehicles. It provides figures between 1987 and 1999 and it shows that the number of privately owned vehicles increased significantly over this period.

(The next two paragraphs describe the trend in more detail and highlight it with data from the graph.)

Between 1987 and 1991, this rise was gradual. For example there were just under 500 vehicles per million of the population in 1987 and this figure rose to 1,000 in 1992.

However, over the next eight years the increase was much greater and between 1992 and 1999, there was a sharp rise in vehicle ownership. By the end of 1999, there were just over 4,000 vehicles per million of the population.

(The final sentence draws a simple conclusion from the data.)

Judging from the data in this graph, the trend is likely to continue in the future.

(122 words)

Sample answer 2
This is a full answer.

(The first two sentences form the opening paragraph that states what the chart shows and describes the main trends.)

The chart shows the changes in the sales of video material / DVDs, games software and CDs around the world in billions of dollars over a three-year period. It can be seen that the sales of videos / DVDs and games software have increased, while the sales of CDs have gone down slightly.

(The next two paragraphs describe the trends in more detail and highlight them with data from the chart.)

Between 2000 and 2003, the sale of videos and DVDs rose by approximately 13 billion dollars. In 2000, just under 20 billion dollars worth of these items were sold, but in 2003, this figure had risen to a little over 30 billion dollars.

The sales of games software also rose during this period, but less sharply. Sales increased from about 13 billion dollars in 2000 to just under 20 billion dollars three years later. By contrast, during the same time period, the sale of CDs fell from 35 billion dollars in 2000 to about 32.5 billion dollars in 2003.

(152 words)

Sample answer
(The first sentence introduces the topic of the pie chart and graph.)

The pie chart shows the worldwide distribution of sales of Coca-Cola in the year 2000 and the graph shows the change in share prices between 1996 and 2001.

(The second paragraph describes the pie chart. As there is not a lot of data in the pie chart, it is possible to mention it all.)

In the year 2000, Coca-Cola sold a total of 17.1 billion cases of their fizzy drink product worldwide. The largest consumer was North America, where 30.4 per cent of the total volume was purchased. The second largest consumer was Latin America. Europe and Asia purchased 20.5 and 16.4 per cent of the total volume respectively, while Africa and the Middle East remained fairly small consumers at 7 per cent of the total volume of sales.

(The third paragraph describes the graph and outlines the trend over the five-year period. Note that not all the data is mentioned. No obvious conclusion can be drawn from the data.)

Since 1996, share prices for Coca-Cola have fluctuated. In that year, shares were valued at approximately $35. Between 1996 and 1997, however, prices rose significantly to $70 per share. They dipped a little in mid-1997 and then peaked at $80 per share in mid-98. From then until 2000 their value fell consistently but there was a slight rise in mid-2000.

(166 words)

UNIT 7 Ignorance is bliss

1 b

2 a

3 The main idea is in the first sentence.

4 The answer is **c** because the paragraph is giving advice and recommends that teachers do this.

IELTS task

The key words in the headings are:

i extra-curricular (a common term meaning 'outside the normal curriculum')

ii independent

iii who / responsible / learning

iv resources (equipment/facilities supplied by the college)

v teaching styles

The answers are:

Paragraph A – heading **ii**

Paragraph B – heading **iv**

LANGUAGE CHECK PAGE 47

1 When I was a Form 4 student, my favourite teacher was Mrs Huxley who taught History and English. I remember she always wore very bright colours and she used to make us laugh by acting out some of the scenes from the history books. Mrs Huxley didn't bore us like other teachers because she was so entertaining. Also, you could always tell that she had done a lot of preparation before each class, which made us feel special.

Since I became a teacher myself, I have thought about Mrs Huxley a lot. She has left the school now and I wonder if she realises that her old students haven't forgotten her!

2 a have thought / has left / haven't forgotten
   b was / taught / wore / used to make /
      didn't bore / could / made   **c** had done

3 1 b   2 a   3 c

4 *Sample answer*
   When I was a student at South College, my least favourite teacher was Mr Finn, who lectured in Graphics and Fine Art. I remember he always gave us lots of homework and he used to shout a lot. Mr Finn didn't believe in groupwork and he never gave us any personal help. I could tell that he had never taught

before because he was so dull. Unfortunately, I haven't taken any interest in Art since that time.

5 a took — simple past (past event now finished)

   b has taken — present perfect (long past event, not finished)

   c did you come — simple past question

   d expected / had expected — simple past / past perfect (the expectation came before the completed course – one past event preceding another past event)

   e have lived — present perfect (past long-term situation related to present situation)

   f Have you applied — present perfect (recent past)

   g had already left — past perfect (one past event preceding another)

WRITING PAGES 48–49

1 a low-tech (equipment)
   b practical (course/approach)
   c optional (course)
   d old-fashioned (methods/approach/course/ equipment)
   e relaxed (approach/lecturer)
   f collaborative (learning/approach/methods)
   g passive (students)

4

	picture A	*picture B*
furniture	old-fashioned	modern
appearance	teacher smart – suit and tie	teacher casual – no tie
teaching/ learning style	formal – whole class, lecture	informal – individual, friendly
behaviour	passive	active

5 a formal   **b** rows   **c** different   **d** groups
   e together/collaboratively

6 *Sample paragraph*
   The way teachers dress and the clothes they wear have also changed a lot. Teachers used to be very smart. Male teachers often wore a suit and a tie and female teachers liked to wear suits sometimes too. But trends have changed and many teachers seem to dress quite casually. They even wear jeans sometimes, although many people still don't like this.

7 b independent / individual **c** exams
d theoretical **e** written **f** passive

8 *Possible answers*
exams – fairer / more objective / sense of achievement
discovery and research – more meaningful to student / less passive / easier to remember

9 *Sample answer*
Students can be assessed in a number of ways but I think the fairest form of assessment is testing. If students have to do examinations, they cannot easily cheat, whereas continuous assessment is difficult to mark and monitor fairly. Generally, examinations give more reliable results than other forms of assessment.

Some education systems emphasise discovery learning, while others tend to spoon feed their students. In my view, it is better to learn things yourself, through your own experiences, because you are more likely to remember what you have learnt. Also, discovery learning is less passive than rote learning and, therefore, more enjoyable.

SPEAKING PAGE 50

1

/ɪd/	/d/	/t/
attended	*played*	*kept*
expected	arrived	fixed
	spilled	bumped
	turned	laughed
	enjoyed	promised

IELTS TEST PRACTICE PAGES 51–53

1 £150 **2** reference number **3** Additional English
4 two/2 weeks **5** accommodation
6 three/3 months **7** academic year **8** vi **9** ix
10 vii **11** viii **12** iii **13** i

UNIT 8 Fit as a fiddle

LISTENING PAGE 54

2 a toe **b** ankle **c** ribs **d** shoulder **e** throat
f wrist **g** elbow **h** neck **i** back **j** knee

2 a heart — single organ which pumps blood through the body
— sits next to the left lung in your chest
— keeps the blood in circulation

b lungs — the body's breathing organs
— in the upper chest
— ensure the body gets oxygen

c stomach — large single organ
— near the waist
— digests food

d brain — organ controlling thought, movement, speech, feeling and emotion
— in your head

4 1 b **2** d **3** g **4** h **5** e **6** a

5 2 fingers – very painful
3 disc, back – it feels stiff
4 elbow – it really hurts, it's killing me
5 ankle – twisted my ankle, swelling, sore
6 throat – sore throat, feel a bit rough

RECORDING SCRIPT CD1 track 21

Conversation 1
Girl: Gee! What've you done to yourself?
Man: Oh, it's too stupid for words. I hit my toe with a hammer!
Girl: Ooh! That must've really hurt! What does it feel like now?
Man: It feels like a bad burn. It's agony.
Girl: Oh! You poor old thing!

Conversation 2
Girl: I can't believe anyone would actually do that!
Man: Yes, it does seem pretty stupid, doesn't it?
Girl: But I suppose young children are capable of anything and their fingers are just small enough to fit into a power point.
Man: They can get a lethal shock, you know. It's extremely dangerous and very painful.

Conversation 3
Doctor: Come in, Mrs Johnson. What can I do for you this evening?
Woman: Well, doctor, I think I've slipped a disc in my back or something.
Doctor: How did you manage that?
Woman: Well I bent down to pick up a box at work and then I just couldn't move … couldn't stand up.
Doctor: And what does it feel like now?
Woman: Well, I can just about walk, but it feels very stiff.

Conversation 4
Coach: Are you OK, Jack?
Boy: Not really! That big bloke – Number 7 on the other team – he tripped me up and I fell on my elbow. If I try to move my arm it really hurts.

Coach: Let's get you off the field and have a look. … Hum … it looks as if you may have actually broken <u>it</u>.
Boy: Yeah! It feels as if I have! <u>It's killing me</u>!

Conversation 5

Mrs Marks: Come in, Mr Fielder.
Mr Fielder: Hello, Mrs Marks!
Mrs Marks: Now, Mr Fielder, as you know, all accidents at work have to be reported to the supervisor. So can you tell me exactly how this injury occurred?
Mr Fielder: Well, I slipped, you see. The floor must have been wet or something and my <u>ankle</u> gave way and I just went flying.
Mrs Marks: And where did this happen?
Mr Fielder: In the corridor. Outside the men's toilets!
Mrs Marks: Any serious injury?
Mr Fielder: Well, I've <u>twisted my ankle</u> and there's some <u>swelling</u>. <u>It's pretty sore.</u>

Conversation 6

Man: You're sneezing a lot today.
Woman: Yes … I think it's hay fever. And I've got a <u>sore throat</u>.
Man: Either that or your immune system is weak.
Woman: Yes. I <u>feel a bit rough</u>. Maybe I should take some vitamin pills.
Man: Good idea. More vitamin C is what you need! You should look after yourself.

Step up to IELTS SPEAKING PAGE 55

For the recording script, please go to
www.cambridge.org/elt/stepup

LANGUAGE CHECK PAGE 56

1 a would b will c would d will e would

2 a can b could not / couldn't c can't
   d Can't you…? e could not / couldn't f can't
   g could not / couldn't

WRITING PAGE 57

1 a the ageing population
   b children under the age of ten
   c the number of births per 1,000 of the population
   d an increase in the spread of malaria in Africa

2 a The cost of theatre tickets remained fairly stable between (the years) 2000 and 2003.
   b The number of hours of sunshine per day fluctuated between January and June.
   c The amount of pollution caused by cars has fallen slightly over the past 35 years.
   d The percentage of women in managerial positions has risen steadily since 1995.

3 a There was little change in the cost of theatre tickets between 2000 and 2003.
   b There was some fluctuation in the number of hours of sunshine per day between January and June.

   c There has been a slight fall in the amount of pollution caused by cars over the past 35 years.
   d There has been a steady rise in the percentage of women in managerial positions since 1995.

Step up to IELTS LISTENING PAGE 58

1 Switzerland
2 (basic) medical attention
3 Geneva Convention
4 war
5 against the law
6 white and green / green and white
7 preserve life
8 protect the victim
9 falling/falls
10 poisoning/poisons

RECORDING SCRIPT CD 1 tracks 23–24

Questions 1–6

Chairperson: Good afternoon, everyone. We're delighted to welcome today a representative from the Red Cross, Mr John Francis, who is going to talk to us about the work of the organisation and about some basic aspects of First Aid.
John Francis: Thank you, Mr Bloom. Well, I'd like to start by giving you some background and then talk about what you would learn on one of our courses. Er, is everyone familiar with the work of the Red Cross?

The Red Cross movement was started by a man called Jean Henri Dunant who was <u>a businessman from Switzerland</u>. His interest in the condition of innocent people caught up in war began in 1859 when he witnessed the effects of a very grim battle in Italy. At the time, he organised all the villagers to help the wounded soldiers and make sure they had food and <u>basic medical attention</u>. A few years later, in 1864, the same gentleman, together with four Swiss colleagues, organised a conference which laid the foundations for the now famous organisation. This was the First <u>Geneva Convention</u>.

So that Red Cross workers could always be recognised, they created their own emblem, rather like a country has its own flag. They chose a red cross on a white background.

The Red Cross operates in just about every country of the world, helping people caught up in famine and <u>war</u> and the emblem is internationally recognised as a symbol of protection and neutrality.

So concerned are the organisers of the Red Cross about the importance of their emblem that it is, in fact, protected by the laws of the Geneva Convention. Sometimes we find that the red cross has been used as a decorative symbol or to indicate first aid stations but this is actually *wrong* because using the emblem for anything other than the international organisation is actually <u>against the law</u>. Even though we tend to associate a red cross with hospitals and medical treatment … which, in a way, isn't surprising, … in Australia, as in many countries, the recognised symbol for first aid and medical centres is not a red cross on a white background but, in fact, a <u>white cross on a green background</u>.

Questions 7–10

John Francis: Now that's the global picture. But what about the local scene? I work for the Australian Red Cross and my job is to train people in basic first aid, which is the name we give to the initial care of the sick or injured.

There are four aims of First Aid, known as the four P's. They are, first and foremost, <u>to preserve life</u>. That is the number one objective of the first aider. Then, the second aim is <u>to protect the victim</u> especially if the victim is actually unconscious. The third 'P' is to prevent the condition from getting worse and lastly to promote recovery. So that's <u>preserve life, protect the victim</u>, prevent things from worsening and promote recovery. And we'll be looking at all of those in some detail during the course.

As a trained First Aider, you could be called upon at any time because accidents invariably happen when they are least expected. Unfortunately, by far the most common cause of injury in our country is on the road, where motor vehicle accidents account for 45% of all accidents. This is followed – and you may be surprised to hear this – by people <u>falling</u> – falling out of windows or trees, falling off walls or simply falling over. <u>Falls account for 21% of all accidents.</u> Then there are accidents that happen at work where machinery is used. They account for 15% of the injuries. In Australia, water is unfortunately another big cause for concern. Each year many

people drown in swimming pools or at the beach and 7% of accidental injuries are related to water. Another cause of injury is <u>poisoning</u>. Our houses are full of products and chemicals for cleaning the floor or killing insects in the garden. Small children are particularly vulnerable here because they cannot read the warnings on the bottles and so <u>poisoning accounts for 5% of injuries</u>.

Now, as a first aider you need a basic understanding of what the human body consists of and how it works. So we are going to start by looking at the organs …

IELTS TEST PRACTICE PAGES 59–61

1	ix	7	(dangerous) myths
2	v	8	buildings
3	iii	9	$2 / two dollars (per/a head)
4	iv	10	health budget / money for health
5	i	11	health
6	vi	12	'burden of disease'
		13	lowland (areas)
		14	28(%) / twenty eight (per cent)

UNIT 9 The driving force

SPEAKING PAGE 62

2 '<u>I prefer travelling by bike</u> (as) it's much easier. In my town… well… <u>it's very difficult to park</u> (because of) all the traffic and parking regulations. I hate wasting time driving around looking for a place (so) I usually take my bike.'

3 *As* and *because* clauses introduce a reason, while *so* clauses introduce the result.

4 a As b so c because d as/since

5 a I'm a vegetarian, so I don't believe in killing animals for food.
   As/since I'm a vegetarian, I don't believe in killing animals for food.
   I'm a vegetarian because I don't believe in killing animals for food.

  b I'm a little short-sighted, so I sometimes need to wear my glasses.
   Since/as I'm a little short-sighted, I sometimes need to wear my glasses.
   I sometimes need to wear my glasses because I'm a little short-sighted.

  c I don't like busy cities because I spent a lot of time in the countryside when I was a child.
   As/since I spent a lot of time in the countryside when I was a child, I don't like cities.
   I spent a lot of time in the countryside when I was a child, so I don't like cities.

  d I hired a large car in Australia because the distances are huge and petrol is relatively cheap.
   The distances are huge in Australia and petrol is relatively cheap, so I hired a large car.
   As/since the distances are huge in Australia and petrol is relatively cheap, I hired a large car.

  e I've lost my umbrella, so I'll buy a new one.
   I'll buy a new umbrella, because I've lost my old one.
   As/since I've lost my umbrella, I'll buy a new one.

WRITING PAGES 63–64

2 a expensive day is Friday.
  b most expensive day is Sunday.
  c least
  d a little more expensive / a little higher

7 a but b Similarly c However d whereas
  e On the other hand f overall/generally/ predictably g although

9 *Sample answer*

The chart shows which driving skills a sample of drivers rated as most difficult.

Predictably, they found parking the most difficult driving skill. Almost fifty per cent of the drivers selected this. The second most difficult skill for them was reversing. Surprisingly, they also considered it hard to keep to the speed limit. Twenty-five per cent of drivers rated this as a difficult skill, whereas they found hill starts considerably less difficult.

Obviously there are many other driving skills, but overall the sample of drivers rated anything else as much less challenging than these four skills.

READING PAGE 65

a The passage divides at the end of the third paragraph. The second part starts 'But what about the solutions?'

b The first part mentions the problems of pollution caused by cars, and the second part offers solutions.

Step up to IELTS READING PAGE 66

Step 1

a *use* and *purposes*

b *journeys to work, the shops or just to enjoy ourselves*

Step 2

a The passage says that advertisers present a glamorised view of cars.

b It means neither: there is no comparison with other products.

Step 3

a *stopped* and *new roads*

b No. *demands for new roads*

c False

IELTS Task

1 T	2 NG	3 F	4 F
5 NG	6 T	7 F	8 NG

9 awareness

10 pollution

11 industries

12 bicycles

13 air

IELTS TEST PRACTICE PAGE 67

1 cart (or) wagon (*both needed*)

2 Scotland

3 taxis

4 horseless carriages

5 bicycle

6 farmers

7 magazine

8 Ford (Motor) Company/Co

9 big (and) expensive (*both needed*)

10 93/ninety-three minutes/mins

RECORDING SCRIPT CD 1 tracks 25–26

Questions 1–5

Presenter: Today, many people own a car and cars have become a common sight around the world. But how did all this come about? In our report today, Jeremy Pemberton gives us a brief history of the motor car.

Jeremy: Well, the first thing you should know is that no single individual was responsible for the invention of the car, or 'automobile' as we call it in the States. The important thing to remember is that the car developed slowly, over time, as hundreds of people sought to produce a motorised vehicle. This means that it's hard to say exactly when the car originated.

The name 'automobile' dates back to a drawing of a carriage mounted on four wheels that was designed by a 14th-century Italian painter named Martini. The name that he gave it, 'automobile', is half Greek ('auto' – meaning 'self') and half Latin ('mobile' – meaning 'moving'). 'Car', on the other hand, comes from a Latin word, 'carrus', meaning <u>'cart' or 'wagon'</u>. Add to that all the French words associated with cars, such as 'chauffeur', 'chassis' and 'garage', and you can start to see how complex the history is.

It's believed that the first electric-powered road vehicle was built in about 1839, in <u>Scotland</u>, by a man called Robert Anderson. The concept of an electrical engine that could start immediately and run quietly was very attractive at that time – as indeed it is now! The first designs were not very successful, though. Later, there were some improvements to these and this led to the appearance of electric <u>taxis</u> on the streets of London in the late 1800s. But they too didn't last long because electric batteries were still heavy, unreliable, and needed recharging after a short run. It's odd to think that we're just going back to solving some of these problems now.

The first real automobiles were very much like motorised versions of horse-drawn vehicles and were referred to as <u>'horseless carriages'</u>. However, there is a much stronger link between cars and bicycles. Many pioneers in the car world were people who were experienced in manufacturing bicycles. In fact, the best place to buy a really fine car in the early 1900s was at the local <u>bicycle</u> shop.

Questions 6–10

Jeremy: There is a common belief that the car is an American invention. But the American car inventors came on the scene relatively late and, while some succeeded, most failed. Then, along came Henry Ford.

Ford was born in 1863. His parents were <u>farmers</u> who had travelled to America from Ireland, but their son disliked the rural lifestyle and in 1879, when he was sixteen years old, he left home and walked to Detroit to find a job. He worked as an apprentice in a machine shop and, in his spare time, he built an internal-combustion engine from plans he found in a <u>magazine</u>. It had bicycle wheels, and was steered by a tiller. It had no brakes or reverse gear and was so noisy that the public hated it.

Some years later, in 1896, he built his first vehicle that was bigger, more powerful, and much faster. It was called the 'quadricycle'. This proved more popular. He was actually able to sell it and raise money for further experiments. During the next several years, Ford continued to refine his passenger vehicles.

Finally, in 1903, he produced an automobile he was ready to market, and so he formed the <u>Ford Motor Company</u>. Ford first brought out the Model A: a small car with an eight-horsepower engine, which sold for US$850. The next year, the Model B Ford was added, which sold for $2,000. In 1906, Ford added the Model K, which Ford lost money on because it was <u>big and expensive</u>. At this point he decided to concentrate on a light, simple model that could be sold inexpensively.

The new design was called the Model T – easy to operate and repair. Customers responded to the advantages of the Model T, and production increased. Gradually Ford found a better, faster way to build cars and in 1914 he opened the world's first auto assembly line. Suddenly, a car could be turned out in <u>93 minutes</u>. By 1924, half of the cars in the world were Fords. The Model T sold for US$290 and profits piled up.

Henry Ford did not create the automobile but it was he who led the manufacturing revolution. He said he would ensure that just about everyone had a car. He kept his word and life has never been the same since.

UNIT 10 *The silver screen*

LISTENING PAGE 68

3 1 H-O-N-O-L-U-L-U
   2 acting (and) dancing
   3 1.77m
   4 1983
   5 thriller
   6 Thunder
   7 Best Actress
   8 divorced / got divorced from
   9 singing

RECORDING SCRIPT CD 2 track 2

Steve: Hi, Miranda. Have you found a biography of Nicole Kidman?

Miranda: Yeah, Steve, well, I've got a couple of things here that I took off the internet so let's see if we can get down some basic details about her first.

Steve: OK, well, we know that she's Australian.

Miranda: Well, that's her nationality, but look at what it says here. She lived in Australia from the age of four, but she was born in Honolulu.

Steve: That's interesting. That's in Hawaii, isn't it? So how do you spell Honolulu?

Miranda: <u>H-O-N-O-L-U-L-U</u>.

Steve: OK, got that.

Miranda: It says that she was very interested in acting as a child. Although her parents were quite strict and worked in politics.

Steve: Mmm.

Miranda: She had to talk about politics at home but <u>her real love was acting and she went to dancing classes</u> from a young age.

Steve: OK. So I'll put those down as her childhood interests.

Miranda: Look, here it says 'the red-headed schoolgirl felt awkward as a child'.

Steve: Well, she's <u>1.77 metres tall</u>.

Miranda: Wow, that *is* tall!

Steve: What about her films?

Miranda: Well, her very first film was called *Bush Christmas*.

Steve: When did she make that? I've never heard of it.

Miranda: In <u>1983</u>. It was about some children looking for a stolen horse, I think.

Steve: But that wasn't the film that made her famous around the world, was it?

Miranda: No, no! That was *Dead Calm* – the scary <u>thriller</u> about the boat. She was only 19 when she made it and she played the part of a woman in her 30s. It was very realistic.

Steve: I think we should jot down some notes about her marriage to Tom Cruise. How did she meet him?

Miranda: Well, she was at a film festival in Japan when she heard that he wanted to meet her. He was starring in a romantic film and he wanted her to play the leading female role.

Steve: Did she get it?

Miranda: Yeah – it's called <u>*Days of Thunder*</u>. Apparently, she was worried about her height. She was taller than Tom Cruise. But he didn't mind. He fell in love with her and they got married in 1990.

Steve: Since then, she's just become more and more famous, hasn't she?

Miranda: Oh, yeah.

Steve: Has she received any awards?

Miranda: Um. Let's see. Yes – she received the <u>Golden Globe Award for Best Actress</u> in the thriller called *To Die For*.

Steve: OK. We can note that down. Does she always star in the same type of film?

Miranda: No, no, she's performed in many different films.

Steve: So, coming up to the present … <u>she and Tom got divorced in 2001</u>, didn't they?

Miranda: Yeah, and <u>since then she's been doing some singing</u>. Oh, and she's won another Golden Globe Award for her film *Moulin Rouge*.

4 a lived; was born   (simple past; passive)
   b didn't; fell; got married (simple past neg; simple past; passive with *got*)
   c she's/she has performed (present perfect)

SPEAKING PAGE 69

2 **a** science fiction **b** comedy **c** thriller
d romance **e** musical **f** cartoon / animated film
g western **h** horror

READING PAGE 70

2 a

Step up to IELTS READING PAGE 71

1–3 B, E, F   6 False   9 Not Given
4 Not Given   7 True   10 C
5 False   8 True

IELTS TEST PRACTICE PAGE 73

Sample answer
(Opening paragraph gives factual information about the popularity of the cinema, using examples.)

The cinema has been a popular form of entertainment for many decades. Even the silent films of the early twentieth century were loved by audiences around the world. Hollywood is now an enormous business and film stars like the Australian actress Nicole Kidman earn millions of dollars.

(Second paragraph focuses on the advantages of DVD and video.)

People think that going to the cinema will become out of date because of the increase in the production of DVDs and videos. It's certainly true that we can all stay at home now and watch films in comfort. Also, the cost of these films is cheaper for a big family than going to the cinema. Young people enjoy spending a night at home and watching a DVD or video. And small children adore videos because they can watch them over and over again.

(Third paragraph provides evidence to show that cinema is still very popular and explains why.)

However, the cinemas in my home country are still full every weekend and when a new film is released we are all very keen to go and watch it. In fact, many small cinemas have been rebuilt and we can now go to large centres that have six or eight cinema screens and show up to ten different films a night. An evening out at the cinema is fun and some films, particularly horror and science fiction films, are much better on the big screen.

(Final paragraph sums up.)

So it seems that we are enjoying both the cinema and the facilities that technology can offer us and that each of these has its merits. In my view, people will never stop going to the cinema but they will watch DVDs as well.

(260 words)

UNIT 11 *The written word*

READING PAGES 74–75

3 Topic: Holiday reading

4 Main idea: The first and last sentences

5 At the beginning and end – it is restated.

6 **a** lawyer (reading boxes of files)
b doctors (reading patients' notes and medical journals)
c literary journalists (reading books for review)

Whether students agree with the writer's view depends on their preferences for reading. It is helpful to consider a personal view because students then interact with the passage and build on ideas. They also need to read widely and develop ideas for the Writing and Speaking parts of the test.

7 Topic: Logophilia or love of words
Main idea: A person who 'suffers' from it can be easily recognised.
Development: Examples of how it can be recognised.

8 The present simple is used because the actions are habitual, and repetition of the structure reinforces this.

9 In paragraph A you could say *for lawyers / for doctors / for literary journalists*. Parallel structure doesn't have to be a verb structure. It will probably improve the paragraph because, at the moment, the paragraph contains a mix of singular and plural professionals.

10 books are good for you
Things that help people recover from flu are not listed in sequential order, but in the order 3, 4, 1, 2. The last two sentences add humour and reinforce the point about books being good for us.

11 1 D   2 B   3 A

LANGUAGE CHECK PAGE 76

1 regularly ask; eagerly take up surreptitiously/sneakily/casually; lean over; happily/gladly linger

2

	adverb	opposite
a expected	expectedly	unexpectedly
b rapid	rapidly	slowly
c wide	widely	narrowly
d happy	happily	unhappily
e deliberate	deliberately	accidentally
f usual	usually	unusually
g final	finally	firstly / initially
h angry	angrily	calmly
i good	well	badly

3 a accidentally b happily/usually/finally
  c deliberately/usually d rapidly
  e unexpectedly f well g widely/usually
  h unexpectedly/unusually

4 *Possible answers*
  a The woman accidentally knocked over a glass of water/juice.
  b The child angrily kicked the other child.
  c The driver stupidly/dangerously drove through a red light.
  d She picked up the broken glass carefully.

WRITING PAGE 77

1 The benefits of writing in an office rather than at home.

2 Feedback can be given on work.
  The stresses of the job are appreciated, so colleges have greater understanding when things go wrong.

4 *Sample answer*
  Cartoons are popular in many countries. The main advantage is that they are illustrated. This makes them easier to read than books, which is why young people like them a lot. Next, they are usually bright and colourful. Finally, they are short, simple and easy to understand. All in all, there are good reasons why people enjoy reading cartoons.

5 a Topic: Children's books/reading
    Main idea: Children enjoy reading these days.
    Supporting points: increases independence
                       uses imagination
                       helps understand the world

  b *Possible answers*
    At asterisks: 'Sitting in a comfortable place and reading by themselves increases their confidence.' 'Children are extremely imaginative and it is important to provide them with an outlet for this.' 'For example, many ideas and experiences can be gained through reading stories about imaginary characters.'

  c 'For these and many other reasons, it is important to encourage children to read as widely as possible.'

6 *Sample answer*
  These days it seems that people have too little time to read because they are so busy. It is true that people often read when they are travelling. However, travel is so fast now that most people only take newspapers or magazines with them. Then, when they get home after work, there are other distractions. Computers, in particular, have taken a lot of people away from books in the same way that TV occupies many children after school. We should try to spend more time reading but it is not easy.

Step up to IELTS SPEAKING PAGE 78

For the recording script, please go to
www.cambridge.org/elt/stepup

UNIT 12 Down to Earth

SPEAKING PAGE 80

1	1 b	3 f	5 h	7 g
	2 a	4 e	6 c	8 d

Step up to IELTS LISTENING PAGES 81–82

a waste water (*not 'water from animals' cages', which is four words*)

b lawns and gardens (*must have both words*)

c $70,000 (*must include dollar symbol*)

RECORDING SCRIPT CD 2 track 6

Interviewer: We've got John Partridge from the Sydney Zoo on the line to talk to us about what they're doing for the environment. Good morning, John.

John: Good morning.

Interviewer: Now, I understand that you've developed a new recycling process at the zoo. Can you tell us about it?

John: Yes, certainly. Well … thanks to some innovative technology, all the <u>waste water</u> – that's the water used when we wash out the animals' cages – is being recycled.

Interviewer: Can you tell us about the process?

John: Well, we've developed a technique for removing all the bacteria and the disease-causing organisms from the waste water by passing it through some plastic fibres.

Interviewer: Is the water clean enough to drink?

John: No, it's not being recycled as drinking water. But thanks to this technique we are managing to re-use all the waste water on the <u>lawns and gardens</u>.

Interviewer: How much did this project cost to introduce?

John: The total system cost 2.2 million dollars, but we have already <u>seen a saving of $70,000</u> in water costs since it was introduced.

Interviewer: That's marvellous!

1 Australia

2 to share experiences

3 waste management

RECORDING SCRIPT CD 2 track 7

Interviewer: If you've ever wondered what 'Clean up the World' was all about, now's your chance to find out. With us in the studio tonight is Melissa Young to tell us about the association. Melissa, welcome!

Melissa: Thank you.

Interviewer: Tell us, where did the idea for 'Clean up the World' come from?

Melissa: Well, it's actually the brainchild of the <u>people who started the movement known as 'Clean up Australia', which has been going in Australia</u> for some ten years now.

Interviewer: And what are the objectives of the organisation?

Melissa: Well … we have three main objectives. We felt we'd gained so much experience in Australia that we wanted <u>to share experiences</u> with people from other nations.

Interviewer: Right!

Melissa: Secondly, we aim to bring people together, people from all corners of the globe, to undertake simple activities that will benefit their local environments.

Interviewer: Right … so you want <u>to share experiences</u> and you want to bring people together at the local level.

Melissa: Yes, that's right. And thirdly, we want to create an international focus that raises the awareness of governments and industries about local environmental issues, <u>but in particular issues of waste management</u>.

4 A / C / F

RECORDING SCRIPT CD 2 track 8

Interviewer: Right. Well those are all good objectives. Is it working?

Melissa: Yes, indeed it is. Since 1993, more than 40 million volunteers from over 120 countries have participated in 'Clean up the World' each year.

Interviewer: Wow! And what does this actually involve in practical terms?

Melissa: There's a variety of activities and these include health programs, large-scale <u>litter clean-ups</u> – that's where a whole lot of people go out and clean up a park, or a beach or something. Then there are public fund-raising events, such as <u>arranging rock concerts</u>, then there's introducing people to recycling systems, as well as school education programs, and we also spend quite a bit of time <u>talking to the government</u>.

5 C	6 B	7 C	8 F	9 A	10 D

RECORDING SCRIPT CD 2 track 9

Interviewer: Where did it all start?

Melissa: Well, as I think I mentioned, 'Clean up the World' was started in Australia and has been exported to more than 60 per cent of the world's countries, stretching from Algeria to Bolivia, and Greece to Vietnam and we've just <u>welcomed Armenia as our most recent member country</u> to the campaign.

Interviewer: <u>Armenia</u>, welcome aboard! Now … I know you're particularly concerned about waste management issues. Can you give us any statistics about the kind of waste issues that are confronting us globally?

Melissa: Sure. Well, for instance it only takes three months <u>for Americans to throw away enough aluminium</u> …

Interviewer: … I suppose that's in the form of <u>aluminium cans</u> …

Melissa: Yes … enough aluminium to replace the entire US commercial aircraft fleet.

Interviewer: Good heavens! That's phenomenal!

Melissa: Yes. That's a lot of cans. And here's another fact: <u>Western Europe produces around 250 million car tyres a year</u>. All of which have to be disposed of.

Interviewer: Wow! Well, there are a lot of <u>cars in Europe</u> obviously. And I suppose they'd get <u>new tyres</u> every second year or so.

Melissa: Yes, exactly! And then there's the <u>plastic bag</u> problem, which is huge. <u>Here in Australia we use six billion bags each year.</u>

Interviewer: Six billion!

Melissa: Yes … and less than one per cent of them is being recycled.

Interviewer: Really? And they're so bad for marine life, aren't they?

Melissa: They certainly are! Thousands of birds die from eating plastic bags each year. You know, <u>research done in Hawaii found that nine out of ten albatross chicks that had died</u> had swallowed some sort of plastic in one form or another. It's really sad and it would be so easy to avoid this. If people would at least throw them in rubbish bins, instead of dropping them on the ground.

Interviewer: Yes, that shouldn't be so hard.

Melissa: And here's one last fact for you. In the <u>Gulf of Mexico there is an area of 7,700 square miles of sea where absolutely no marine life exists</u>, other than bacteria.

Interviewer: Melissa, thank you for coming on the programme today and for sharing all your facts and figures with us. And good luck with the 'Clean up the World' campaign!

WRITING PAGES 83–84

1 a Although / Even though   b For one thing
  c for another   d but   e As far as the question of
  f is concerned   g so

2 a According to the store manager, it is the customer's responsibility to dispose of the bags in a sensible way.
  b The woman thinks the supermarkets are to blame because they use too many bags.
  c The male customer believes it is best to take a bag to the supermarket and that way he avoids the problem of how to dispose of the bags.

3 *Sample paragraph*
  Even though the supermarkets may feel it is the customer's responsibility to dispose of the bags, I don't believe they can avoid taking some blame. For one thing, they often supply more bags than are needed. One solution is for shoppers to bring their own bags to avoid having to use any plastic bags and this seems a sensible approach.

4 a 2 b 5 c 4 d 1 e 6 f 3

6 *Sample answer*
  Even though the environmentalist movement may want to stop all forms of hunting, there are people, such as professional fishermen, whose livelihood depends on their ability to fish or hunt. Traditional hunters also hunt only for their own survival, or to keep themselves warm, and not with the intention of killing off a species, so perhaps we should accept this. However, I do think it is wrong to kill animals just for amusement, as in the case of fox hunting, for example. I also think it is wrong to use their shell, skin or fur to make things like jewellery or handbags.

7 a Be quiet and stop talking.
  b The bad weather prevented us from going to the beach / stopped us from going …
  c The customs officer stopped / prevented me from importing the wooden fruit bowl.
  d We're trying to stop people from trading in ivory.
  e The green parties want to stop/prevent people from destroying the environment.
  f The company stopped paying tax ten years ago.

IELTS TEST PRACTICE PAGE 85

1 (an) artist
2 (a) businessman
3 (a) scientist
4 museum (in London)
5 discovered (and) named
6 Birds of Australia
7 fur and feathers
8 (a) (wax) crayon
9 by hand / hand-coloured
10 (about) 250

RECORDING SCRIPT CD2 tracks 10–11

Questions 1–6

Presenter: Good evening and welcome to this week's edition of *Radio Art Club*. With us in the studio is Martin Wade, who is an art dealer, and he's here to talk to us about a man called John Gould. Welcome, Martin.

Martin: Good evening.

Presenter: John Gould, if I'm right, was known as the 'Bird Man', but who was he really?

Martin: Well, Gould was a man of many parts. I suppose that first and foremost he was an <u>artist</u>, but he also had a keen eye for business, so we could also call him <u>a businessman</u>, and as well as that he was <u>a scientist</u>.

Presenter: He studied birds, didn't he?

Martin: Yes, that's correct.

Presenter: Right, so we've got <u>an artist, a businessman and a scientist</u> all rolled into one. And why is he famous?

Martin: Well, predominantly because he produced the greatest collection of drawings of Australian birds ever.

Presenter: Can you tell us about his life? What kind of a man was he?

Martin: Now, let's see. He was born in England in 1804 and he lived for 76 years, so he had a comparatively long and productive life. He had no formal education and when he was a young man in the 1820s, he worked as a gardener in Kew Gardens in London and then, because of his interest in animals, he was made <u>curator of a museum</u>, in fact the Zoological <u>Museum</u> in London.

Presenter: Right, so he had quite a few interests.

Martin: Absolutely. He and his wife together. They were both very interested in the discovery of new species of animals.

Presenter: So when did he visit Australia?

Martin: Well … in 1838 Gould and his wife and their eldest son sailed from England, leaving their three youngest children behind with the grandparents!

Presenter: Gracious!

Martin: They travelled around extensively and although they were only there for two years, <u>Gould discovered many new species and he also named them.</u>

Presenter: Yes, he played a significant role, didn't he?

Martin: The family returned to England in August 1840 and took with them hundreds of specimens of animals for their great work which was still to be produced. In fact it took them eight years to produce the full work which was completed in 1848 and published under the simple name of *Birds of Australia*.

Questions 7–10

Presenter: Now, tell us about the drawings themselves. What process did he use to produce the prints of his drawings?

Martin: He used a process known as lithography.

Presenter: Why did he choose this in particular?

Martin: He chose it because he felt it was the best method he could use to accurately reproduce the <u>fur and feathers</u> of the animals.

Presenter: I see. Can you tell us briefly what it involves?

Martin: Yes, certainly. Well first of all the drawing was made onto a flat slab of limestone. In order to do this, he <u>used a wax crayon.</u> You don't need any technical skill to do this, other than an ability to draw.

Presenter: Which John Gould obviously had!

Martin: Yes, that's right. Then when he'd done the first drawing, he wet the stone and applied the ink. Where the stone was wet, the ink didn't stick. That's how he got the outline.

Presenter: Aha!

Martin: Then, the inky picture was transferred to a piece of paper using a special printing press.

Presenter: Simple! Many of the prints are coloured. How did they do this?

Martin: Well, it was a slow and laborious job. Each individual picture <u>was coloured by hand</u>.

Presenter: Right. That must have taken some patience and I suppose that's why the result is so incredible.

Martin: Yes.

Presenter: And how many prints did he produce?

Martin: We think he produced <u>about 250 of each</u>, but there's no way of telling how many have survived the 150 years that have passed since then. Which is why the few examples that we have are so valuable, especially as many of the animals he drew are now extinct.

Presenter: That's absolutely fascinating. Thank you so much for joining us this evening.

Martin: Pleasure.

UNIT 13 Safe as houses

Step up to IELTS LISTENING PAGES 86–87

1

Place where you live	Parts of a building	Building materials	People
apartment	balcony	brick	architect
dwelling	column	concrete	builder
flat	door	mud	carpenter
home°	floor	steel	engineer
house	level	stone	landlord
skyscraper°°	roof	tile	neighbour
	room	wood	tenant
	stairs		
	stilts		
	verandah		
	wall		
	window		

° home = a place where you live, but not an actual building
°° skyscraper = a very tall building, often used as an office rather than a dwelling place

2 *Possible answers*

b House b is on stilts, actually standing in a river. It could be on the Mekong River in a country like Vietnam.

c This is a picture of three skyscrapers. It looks as if it could be in a city like Kuala Lumpur or Hong Kong. Each building has at least 24 floors and may contain apartments or office accommodation. This type of building is typical of many modern cities.

d This is a little one-storey cottage in the countryside. It is made of stone and it has two chimneys. It's probably in a European country where the weather is cold.

e House e is called a chalet and it's made of wood. You would find a house like this in a country in the Alps, such as Switzerland or Austria. The roof is designed to allow the snow to fall off and the windows are small to keep in the heat.

IELTS task

1 bad weather	4 construction
2 beautiful	5 ability to build
3 work	6 climatic conditions

RECORDING SCRIPT CD 2 track 12

Lecturer: Good morning, everyone. Now, today, I'm going to talk to you about the history of building and architecture.

No story is more interesting or impressive than the story of man's progress through the ages, and in particular the activities of human beings in the art of building. Let's have a look at this in some detail.

In very early times, around 50,000 years ago, primitive humans lived in trees and caves, where they found protection from wild beasts and shelter from bad weather. However, these natural shelters were pretty uncomfortable and so humans began to think of ways to construct more permanent dwellings, such as tents and huts.

From these humble beginnings a great variety of architectural styles gradually developed, and we see how humans began to master constructional difficulties and at the same time to achieve aesthetic desires. In other words, we see how they began to create buildings that were not only functional but beautiful as well.

Generally, architecture is concerned with the enclosing of space. Another way of saying this is that architecture is about creating a safe, healthy and pleasant space for the occupants – that is, for the people living and working there. A healthy place in which to live and also in which to work.

There are three basic principles of architecture and I'd like to run over these now. The first is the principle of function: that is, the purpose of the building in question. The second is the principle of construction: how is the building to be built or constructed? And the third, after construction, is artistic expression.

In the course of time, communities of human beings settled in different parts of the world, and often they were able to create distinctive architectural styles, styles which fulfilled the needs and desires of the people of those times. The creation of any architectural style depends upon four things. Firstly, the physical and mental state of the people. Are they happy, are they at war with other tribes? … that sort of thing. The second thing that leads to the creation of a style is their knowledge of how to actually construct a building; in other words, their ability to build. Thirdly, of course, you have to take into account the availability of materials with which to build, and lastly, and this is to my mind the most important, the climatic conditions will play a role. So, for instance, in a cold climate, the priority is to keep out the cold and in a tropical climate, the aim is to stay cool.

7 B   8 E   9 B   10 A

RECORDING SCRIPT CD 2 track 13

Lecturer: I'd like to focus for a moment on the influence of *climate* on architecture. For example, in Greece, where there is a moderate rainfall and strong light, they adopted low-pitched roofs and few window openings. The ancient people of Egypt constructed buildings with flat roofs and small windows as Egypt has a dry climate with bright light. However, in the colder climates of the northern hemisphere – countries like Sweden and Switzerland – they resorted to steep-pitched roofs to allow the snow to run off. And for people living in a river delta where the land is prone to flooding, you will often find houses built on stilts to keep them clear of the water … places such as Vietnam.

So what materials are generally used? Well, stone, brick, concrete and wood have been the traditional building materials, but, from the earliest times, *stone* has generally been chosen for *important* structures because of its durability and workability. The main types of construction are shown here in your handout. Have a look at the illustrations on page one. Firstly, we have the post and lintel, made out of stone. The posts, or

columns as they are also known, stand perpendicular to the ground. You can then lay another stone across the top of two columns and this is called a lintel or beam. However, for this type of construction to work, it's important that the columns are close to one another and that the space between the columns is not more than twice the width of the two columns. This structure was very popular in ancient Egypt and Greece.

Another very common technique in building was the arch. An arch can span a wider space than a post and lintel, and is remarkably strong. The Romans were very keen on this form of structure and you will find Roman arches still standing today, as strong as when they were first built. At the top of the arch is a stone known as the keystone, which provides the arch with its strength. Roman arches were never pointed at the top. The pointed arch, known as the Gothic arch, came some time later.

These days, large buildings are usually built with reinforced concrete. Unlike the buildings of the ancient Greeks and Romans …

Step up to IELTS ACADEMIC AND GENERAL TRAINING WRITING PAGES 89–90

Sample answer

Every city has its architectural character, but the similarities between cities are more obvious these days than in the past. In my opinion, one reason for this is the high price of land.

In most large cities, land is scarce and consequently it is very valuable. This has led to the construction of tall buildings which occupy only a small area of land while providing lots of floor space where people can live or work. Buildings of this type are made of concrete and steel and can be built comparatively quickly using pre-fabricated materials. They do not use local materials, such as stone, timber or brick, which used to give cities their individual character. In consequence many cities now look very much the same and you might not know whether you were in Brisbane, Bangkok or Berlin when you are on the street.

While I realise that we cannot stand in the way of progress, I believe that cities should try to keep some individuality. For example, in Paris it is prohibited to build very tall buildings in the centre of the city, as this would spoil the overall appearance of the skyline.

Other cities have chosen to design unique buildings to ensure they look different. The twin towers in Kuala Lumpur or the Opera House in Sydney are examples of this approach, and I agree with this kind of initiative.

All in all, although it is regrettable that modern cities look similar, I tend to feel that this is unavoidable. However, it can be argued that, even if the buildings are similar, cities will maintain their own character as a result of cultural diversity, the terrain and the climate, which ultimately determine how people live.

(286 words)

IELTS TEST PRACTICE PAGE 91

Sample answer
(Introduction: mention that public buildings exist in all cities and towns, large and small, e.g. post office, court house, places of worship, theatre)

A public building is a building that belongs in some way to the state. The number of public buildings in any town or village will depend on the size of that community and its needs. For example, you will usually find a town hall of some sort, a school and a place of worship at the least. In larger communities there will be a police station, law courts, a library and maybe a theatre funded by the state.

(Pros: city pride, beautiful to look at, useful/necessary buildings, create a city centre.)

The desire to build impressive buildings is not new. The ancient cities of the Middle East and South America were designed with large public buildings to impress visitors and enemies and give a sense of pride. In modern times, outstanding public buildings still create a great sense of local and national pride. They are what gives a city its character and they form a social centre, a place where people like to meet.

(Cons: waste of public money, intimidating, nationalistic. Give opinion on whether they stop us from building houses or whether they can be compatible.)

However, some people argue that governments have constructed unnecessary, and sometimes ugly, buildings simply to make themselves feel important. I tend to feel that such buildings may be a waste of public money but I am not sure we can claim that they prevent houses from being built, because these governments have often ensured that adequate housing was also available. Houses and public buildings can exist side by side.

(Conclusion – sum up the two parts to the answer. Leave the reader thinking.)

The answer lies in finding the right balance. We want to feel pride in our town, but we also want our citizens to have comfortable homes. It is hard to please everyone.

(252 words)

UNIT 14 On the face of it

LISTENING PAGE 93

1–2

speaker	feeling	words used
1	disappointed	all I got / let down
2	nervous / anxious / worried	won't sleep / shaking / relieved when it's over
3	excited	really looking forward / can't wait
4	shocked / stunned / surprised	couldn't believe it
5	angry / annoyed	fed up / that's the last time / furious
6	suspicious	up to something / something going on

RECORDING SCRIPT CD 2 track 14

Speaker 1: I did what Mr Winton suggested and I read all the right articles for that sociology assignment and then <u>all I got</u> was a grade D. <u>I felt really let down</u> after all my efforts.

Speaker 2: Well, I've done heaps of preparation for the music presentation I'm doing tomorrow but I still <u>won't sleep</u> tonight. I'll probably get up in the middle of the night and start practising. Look at me – <u>I'm shaking</u> at the thought. <u>I'll be relieved</u> when it's all over.

Speaker 3: Tom and I are <u>really looking forward</u> to going away for a couple of weeks. We've both worked so hard this term and now <u>I just can't wait</u> to get on that plane!

Speaker 4: My neighbour's always been such a nice, pleasant, friendly person – always ready to lend a helping hand. And then one day I found out that he once spent three years in prison for robbery. <u>I just couldn't believe it.</u>

Speaker 5: They turned up over an hour late, didn't ring or anything, didn't apologise when they arrived. <u>I'm fed up.</u> <u>That's the last time</u> I invite them round for dinner. They didn't say anything about the food, not even a 'thank you', and then they left as soon as they'd finished eating. <u>I'm furious.</u>

Speaker 6: Every time I lend my car to my son it comes back dirty. He says he only wants to drive it to college in the morning, but I think <u>he's up to something</u> else. I don't know where he's going with it but <u>there's something going on.</u> Do you think I should follow him?

4

		words used
Amanda	✔	I get really irritated / can't stand it / don't you hate it
Walid		a bit annoying / doesn't bother

5 A

RECORDING SCRIPT CD 2 track 15

Amanda: Have you ever smoked, Walid?

Walid: No, I've never really wanted to.

Amanda: Mmm. I used to be a smoker but <u>I get really irritated</u> now when I see people smoking in public places.

Walid: Yes, it's <u>a bit annoying in restaurants</u>.

Amanda: Oh, <u>I can't stand it</u> anywhere, even outdoors.

Walid: Really? <u>It doesn't bother me</u>.

Amanda: Don't you hate it at parties, people puffing in your face?

Walid: Not particularly.

6

		words used
other people's views	*in favour of marriage*	happy occasion / celebrate
her parents' views	in favour of marriage	it's important / be very upset
her own views	uncertain / undecided	not so sure / wouldn't bother me

7 B

RECORDING SCRIPT CD 2 track 16

Young woman: People always seem to get excited about a wedding. I guess they feel it's <u>a happy occasion</u> and it's a time when all the family can get together and <u>celebrate</u>. My parents don't *worry* about when I'll get married but I know <u>they think it's important</u> and <u>they'd be very upset</u> if I decided never to do it. As for me, well, <u>I'm not so sure</u>. I'll get married if I find the right person and if he wants to get married but I'm not going to rush into it just to please my parents. I think I'm quite content on my own and <u>it wouldn't bother me</u> if I stayed single.

9 1 C   2 A   3 B   4 C   5 B

RECORDING SCRIPT CD 2 track 17

Hiba: Look at this topic: What do you remember most about your teenage life? <u>I've never had an assignment quite like this before</u>.

Ahmed: No, I know what you mean. Normally we have to go and research something in the library.

Hiba: But this time we've got to produce something from our own personal experience. Still, <u>I guess it's different</u>.

Ahmed: What are you going to write about, Hiba?

Hiba: That's a good question. All sorts of things happened to me when I was a teenager. I know that I argued with my brother a lot ... I felt that my parents didn't understand me ... all that kind of stuff. But <u>those stages are pretty standard</u>, aren't they? <u>Everyone goes through them</u>. And it doesn't mean you were unhappy – quite the opposite in fact.

Ahmed: Yes. I suppose we have to pick on something ... <u>something that 'happened' or an incident</u> perhaps that 'changed' us in some way – made us more independent.

Hiba: Mmmm. Can you think of one, Ahmed?

Ahmed: There's one thing that stands out for me.

Hiba: What's that?

Ahmed: Well, when I was about 16, my father decided that I needed to learn how to look after myself, so he had this crazy idea. He didn't think it was crazy, of course. Even now <u>he tells all his friends what an amazing thing he did</u> and boasts about how it made me the 'man' I am now. Whereas, for me, it was quite different.

Hiba: What happened?

Ahmed: You won't believe this! He drove me into the middle of the desert and left me there. Told me I had to find my own way home. It was like a test of my courage and my ability to deal with a tricky situation.

Hiba: You obviously found your way home.

Ahmed: Yes, I did. I do feel quite good that I made it.

Hiba: There, see. I'm sure he would have come to find you if you hadn't turned up.

Ahmed: I suppose so.

Hiba: <u>I wish I could have had a chance to prove myself like that</u>.

Ahmed: I'd never want to go through it again.

READING PAGES 94–95

1 a Being together in the same place. Often used as a modifier before a noun such as 'communication' or 'interview'.

b It is going to discuss facial expressions in terms of how we understand them.

2 a facial expressions **b** rules **c** culture
   d film / footage **e** read faces
   f system / taxonomy **g** muscular movement
   h action units / facial expressions

3 1 read faces   5 Silvan Tomkins
   2 rules   6 muscular movement
   3 photographs   7 10,000
   4 cultural

Step up to IELTS READING PAGE 96

1 E   2 F   3 C   4 B   5 A   6 D   7 C

UNIT 15 As far as I can see

READING PAGE 98

Sample answers

2 Certain types of AI exist already

↓

Robotics more difficult because
 i cannot navigate
 ii cannot do more than one task at a time
 iii cannot recognise and express emotion – linked with logic

↓

Some very basic attempts e.g. Kismet – facial expressions
Computer with 6 types of emotional recognition

↓

Need true emotions e.g. consciousness and self-awareness – this is unlikely!

3 Basic forms of Artificial Intelligence already exist and scientists are attempting to develop robots that display and recognise emotions. However, there is little likelihood that they will ever be able to produce a robot that is similar to a human being.

Step up to IELTS READING PAGE 99

1 F   2 B   3 E   4 C   5 G   6 C   7 D

WRITING PAGES 100–101

1 <u>This graph</u> shows the change in library use between 1991 and 2000. During <u>this period</u>, there was a gradual fall in the number of people <u>who</u> visited libraries and the number of books <u>which</u> were taken out on loan. <u>This decline</u> was more significant for book loans, <u>which</u> fell from 500 million in 1991 to just under 400 million in 2000. <u>In comparison with this</u>, general library visits fell from 350 million to 300 million <u>over the same period</u>. There was a slight levelling off for <u>both</u> in the last year of the decade.

2 a *this* + noun
 b *it/this* to refer back to what has just been stated
 c *there* to refer back to place
 d *these* to refer back beyond the sentence level
 e *who* as relative pronoun
 f *such* + noun
 g *which* as a connector

3 a these ideas/aims   e this approach
 b this aircraft   f this kind/nature
 c This skill/ability   g this experience
 d These institutions

4 a such a concept
 b such an old-fashioned view
 c such instruments
 d such behaviour

5 a it   f which
 b these things   g such useful facilities
 c this   h make such complaints
 d which
 e this basic equipment

SPEAKING PAGE 102

2 a I'm going to Kenya because my sister's working there.
 b I think I'll probably marry someone kind and hard-working.
 c I think I'll still be in Australia.
 d I'm going to have a party because it's my 21st.
 e I'm going to work for a year in my father's business.

3 *Possible answers*
 a She's going to miss the bus.
 b The teacher won't let him take his exam.

RECORDING SCRIPT CD 2 tracks 18–22

a

Examiner: Do you think that scientists will successfully clone human beings one day?
Student: Yes, I think they will. From what I've read so far, they've already cloned a sheep.
Examiner: How do you think this will affect society?
Student: Well, as far as I can see, it's more a question of ethics than simple science. I think it could be quite harmful to society as a whole. But for medical purposes, I suppose it's OK. I think that's a very hard one to answer.

b

Examiner: Do you think we'll ever use computers to mark language speaking tests?
Student: Gosh, I hope not! If they do, then I think students will feel concerned about fairness – the computer might make mistakes. I mean how can you tell if a computer gets things wrong? Also the exams would become very boring.
Examiner: So you'd prefer to talk to a human being?
Student: Oh, yes, definitely.

c

Examiner: Do you think we'll see robots doing medical operations?

Student: Yes, I think we will. From what I've read, robotics are already involved in … eye operations for instance.

Examiner: How would you feel about having machines performing routine tasks in a hospital?

Student: Fine! I think we'll see a greater reliance on machines in the future. They already have machines which take your blood pressure automatically, every half an hour, after an operation, without a nurse having to come and do it.

d

Examiner: Do you think we'll see hotels being built in space in the foreseeable future?

Student: I'm not sure. Perhaps we will … if you count the International Space Station as a hotel.

Examiner: How do you think this will affect the tourist industry?

Student: Well, I wouldn't see it as a huge threat at this stage. But we do already have a situation where wealthy individuals are prepared to pay enormous sums of money to travel to outer space without performing any useful function when they're there. Just to say they've been there. So I suppose this is a form of holidays in space. It might increase in popularity.

e

Examiner: Do you believe that we'll develop drugs that lengthen our lifespan?

Student: Yes … I mean, any drug that's effective … in curing us of disease or whatever, is lengthening our lifespan, isn't it? But whether we actually want a drug that will make us live forever is another question.

Examiner: How would you feel about taking a drug that promised to do this?

Student: I don't think this will happen in the foreseeable future, but perhaps in 100 years or so. I think it would lead to all sorts of problems. Would anyone really want to live forever? I don't think so.

IELTS TEST PRACTICE PAGE 103

1 Airbus A320

2 legs

3 mirror

4 touch screen

5 teams / a team

6 wind

7 engine

8 flight management computer

9 instruments

10 first officer

RECORDING SCRIPT CD 2 track 23

John: Good morning everyone. My name is John McNally and, as you know, I'm a software engineer. I work very close to Gatwick Airport in Britain and at work we assemble flight simulators, which are used to train aeroplane pilots. So before any pilot is able to get in a real plane and fly it, they have to prove that they can operate all the controls in an aeroplane by flying in a computerised model.

So what does a flight simulator look like? Well, here's a picture of one: the simulator here is a model of a plane called an Airbus A320. As you can see, it's a large, almost round blob or box that moves on – usually six – legs to simulate the movement of an aircraft in the air. The legs tend to be driven by hydraulics but there are some electric ones around. Either way, they operate to simulate the motion – the pitch and roll – of the aircraft. The simulator can move up in the air or stretch, giving the trainee the feeling of flying upwards. At the very front, in the curved area here, is the 'mirror' and this is here so that images can be created that look exactly like an airport or landscape.

Inside, the simulator tends to resemble an actual flight deck in an aircraft. And what happens is that generally the instructor stands or sits behind the trainee and 'positions' the aircraft to any airport or any position on that airport using a touch screen. In this way, the instructor can 'train' the pilot. And there are many tests that the instructor can put the trainee through. He can fail an engine in flight, for example, to test the trainee's ability to react to 'malfunctions'.

How does it do this? Well, the simulator contains many computers, most of which have to communicate with each other. That's my job and I work with many other software experts on this. We work in teams, which vary in size, and each team has a specialist area but all the systems need to know what the other is doing. If the instructor wants to simulate a storm, for example, the flight experts need to know the strength of the winds and if there is any turbulence. At the same time, the navigation people need to know where the storm is, how far away, and place it on the pilot's navigation screen, and the engine experts need their information to ensure a safe passage. In fact, landing an aircraft in rough weather is one of the most difficult things to do and I've seen some very pale people step out of simulators in my time here! It can get very stormy in there!

But trainees don't get into a simulator straight away! There are many different devices used in the training process and this starts on a very simple level. One of the first things a trainee must know is how to input data into the flight management computer. The pilot, on an aircraft, enters information such as 'Current Airport', 'Destination Airport' as well as his route and other things such as the amount of fuel and aircraft weight. This procedure can be learned on a PC. Next, he may need to learn to manage the controls, for example, using the joystick to move up or down or left or right. He gets the 'feel' of these controls and how they impact on the instruments. This can be learned on a 'fixed base' simulator – that's one that doesn't move. Finally, he needs to take off, land and fly in the air during turbulence, etc, so for that he needs a full flight simulator with motion.

Trainee pilots vary in age and ability and so the length of time it takes to train them also varies. Once a pilot has qualified on the simulator they are entitled to fly an aircraft but they are only called a 'first officer' at this stage and must fly under an experienced captain … unless they are an experienced pilot who is simply re-training to fly a different aircraft type.

UNIT 16 Mother tongue

SPEAKING PAGES 104–105

3 The pictures are:
a Egyptian hieroglyphs; b deaf sign language;
c the Japanese characters for *forest* and *sea*;
d *No smoking* in Thai; e the number pi;
f the road sign warning of a railway crossing.

READING PAGE 106

a number of languages / world / estimates varied /
problems / question
*It is difficult to know exactly how many languages
exist today because linguists cannot agree on what
counts as a language.*

b distinction between language and dialect / standard
written language
*Although English is spoken in a number of ways, it
has a standard written form.*

c varieties of speech / dialects / different from each
other
*The dialects of China are quite different from each
other.*

d language planning / official policy / planning issues /
languages and linguistic varieties
*In both developing and developed nations,
governments need to have a policy on how to deal
with issues relating to the languages spoken in that
country.*

e origins of human language / questions / search is
fruitless
*People have wondered for years about the origins of
human language, but the questions remain
unanswered as there is no real way of knowing.*

Step up to IELTS READING PAGE 107

1 Yes 2 No 3 Not given 4 Yes 5 Not given
6 No 7 Yes 8 Not given

WRITING PAGE 108

Sample answer
*(Clear statement followed by a question based on the
premise.)*

Language is linked to the identity of a nation, and
speakers of a common language share many things, but
does this give governments the right to restrict the way
a language is used or taught?

*(Concession made to the 'For' case, but followed by the
'Against' point of view. An example is given which
comments on the likely effectiveness of such a policy.)*

It can be argued that a nation maintains its culture
through its language, and so there is a need to restrict
the use of foreign words and changes in pronunciation.
However, in reality this approach is fruitless, because
language is a living thing and it is impossible to stop it
from changing. This policy has been tried in some
countries, but it never works. People, especially young
people, will use the language that they hear around
them, and which separates them from others; stopping
the use of certain words will only make them appear
more attractive.

*(Puts the case 'Against' governments preventing
spelling reform, but concedes it may be useful.)*

As for spelling, we all know that the English system is
irregular and, I believe, it would benefit from
simplification so that children and other learners do
not waste time learning to read and write. On the other
hand, some people may feel, perhaps rightly, that it is
important to keep the original spelling of words as a
link with the past and this view is also held by speakers
of languages which do not use the Roman alphabet.

*(Puts both sides of the argument about which language
to use in schools.)*

While it is important for people who speak a minority
language to be able to learn and use that language, it is
practical for education to be in a common language.
This creates national pride and links people within the
society. Realistically, schools are the best place for this
to start.

(Ends with a clear statement.)

Ultimately, there is a role for governments to play in
the area of language planning, particularly in
education, but at no time should governments impose
regulations which restrict people's linguistic freedom.

(292 words)

IELTS TEST PRACTICE PAGES 109–111

1 Yes	7 C	13 A
2 Yes	8 C	14 D
3 Not Given	9 C	
4 No	10 B	
5 No	11 A	
6 Not Given	12 B, E, F	

Overview of IELTS Test

Paper	Breakdown	Skills Tested
Listening		
30 minutes + 10 minutes transfer time	4 sections and 40 questions (10 questions in each section)	Listening for: topic / situation / detail / specific information / opinion / main ideas
Academic Reading		
One hour	3 sections, each comprising a text of about 900 words 40 questions	Understanding: topic / situation / detail / specific information / opinion / main and supporting ideas / global ideas / gist
General Training Reading		
One hour	Section 1 – small extracts Section 2 – two texts Section 3 – one long text 40 questions	Understanding: topic / situation / detail / specific information / opinion / main and supporting ideas / global ideas / gist
Academic Writing		
One hour	Task 1: Describing graphic data / a diagram	Describing trends Making comparisons Describing a process / diagram Paragraphing and organisation Language accuracy and range Lexical accuracy and range
	Task 2: Writing an essay	Presenting an argument Supporting a point of view Coherence and cohesion Paragraphing and organisation Language accuracy and range Lexical accuracy and range
General Training Writing		
One hour	Task 1: Writing a letter	Responding appropriately to a stimulus / register / style Paragraphing and organisation Language accuracy and range Lexical accuracy and range
	Task 2: Writing an essay	As for Academic Writing Task 2
Speaking		
11–14 minutes	Part 1: Interview 4–5 minutes Part 2: Long turn 3–4 minutes Part 3: Discussion 4–5 minutes	Responding to questions / talking about oneself Giving a short talk / describing / explaining / reporting Expressing and supporting an opinion / agreeing / disagreeing / speculating Grammar / Vocabulary / Pronunciation

The IELTS Band scale

Band 9 – Expert User
Has fully operational command of the language: appropriate, accurate and fluent with complete understanding.

Band 8 – Very Good User
Has fully operational command of the language with only occasional unsystematic inaccuracies and inappropriacies. Misunderstandings may occur in unfamiliar situations. Handles complex detailed argumentation well.

Band 7 – Good User
Has operational command of the language, though with occasional inaccuracies, inappropriacies and misunderstandings in some situations. Generally handles complex language well and understands detailed reasoning.

Band 6 – Competent User
Has generally effective command of the language despite some inaccuracies, inappropriacies and misunderstandings. Can use and understand fairly complex language, particularly in familiar situations.

Band 5 – Modest User
Has partial command of the language, coping with overall meaning in most situations, though is likely to make many mistakes. Should be able to handle basic communication in own field.

Band 4 – Limited User
Basic competence is limited to familiar situations. Has frequent problems in understanding and expression. Is not able to use complex language.

Band 3 – Extremely Limited User
Conveys and understands only general meaning in very familiar situations. Frequent breakdowns in communication occur.

Band 2 – Intermittent User
No real communication is possible except for the most basic information using isolated words or short formulae in familiar situations and to meet immediate needs. Has great difficulty understanding spoken and written English.

Band 1 – Non User
Essentially has no ability to use the language beyond possibly a few isolated words.

Band 0 – Did not attempt the test
No assessable information provided.

Acknowledgements

The authors and publishers would like to thank the teachers and students who trialled and commented on the material:

Australia: Stephen Heap; China: Wu Ruiling; Greece: Jane Richards; New Zealand: Belinda Hayes; Singapore: Pamela Humphreys; Taiwan: Daniel Sansoni; UK: Jan Benjamin, Paul Bress, Roger Scott, Steve Walsh, Norman Frank Whitby, Peter Whitton; Ukraine: Olena Lesnyak; United Arab Emirates: Lynne Kennedy.

The authors and publishers are grateful to the following for permission to use copyright material in *Step Up to IELTS*. While every effort has been made, it has not been possible to identify the sources of all the material used and in such cases the publishers would welcome information from the copyright owners:

for the information on p. 13, © Australian Sports Commission, reproduced with permission; Dr Rosemary Stanton for the extract on p. 15 adapted from *Food Trivia*; for the article 'Food for Thought', *The Economist*, 7 July, 2001, p. 19, and the extract, 'Paper Money', *The Economist* 22 December 2001, p. 40, and the graph, 'Over a barrel', *The Economist*, 15 December 2001, p. 43, for the graph, 'Road to Prosperity', *The Economist*, 23 June 2001, p. 44, and the graph, 'That's no niche', *The Economist* 22 June 2002, p.44, and the graphs, 'A lot of bottle', and 'Fizzling', *The Economist*, 3 February 2001, p. 45, and the article 'For 80 cents more', *The Economist*, 17 August 2002, p. 59, © The Economist Newspaper Limited; for 'Mekong Magic' on p. 24, adapted from 'Delta Force' by Gary Walsh, published in the *Sydney Morning Herald*, 23 March 2002; for the extract on p. 29, from *The Living Planet*, reprinted by permission of HarperCollins, Publishers Ltd © David Attenborough 1984; John Ibbotson for the article, 'The history of lighthouses', on p. 30, adapted from *Lighthouses of Australia*, published 2001; for the diagrams, 'Zones of the seashore', on p. 32, and the 'Depth zones of the ocean', on p. 33, and the graphs of 'Brisbane / Melbourne climate' on p. 36, from *Amazing Facts about Australian marine life*, © Steve Parish Publishing Pty Ltd.; for the article 'Red Cross' on p. 58, used with permission of the Canadian Red Cross Society; for the text on p. 65, 'On the move Scottish power', adapted from an article by Tony Juniper (Friends of the Earth) published in *BBC Wildlife Magazine*, September 2002; for the text on p. 98, adapted from 'Robots with emotion', published in *Focus Magazine*, November 2001 © Origin Publishing Ltd.; for the text on p. 70 'Bollywood – the Indian Cinema', adapted from *Bollywood – The Indian Cinema Story* by Nasreen Munni Kabir, published by Pan Macmillan, London, August 2002; Ruth Padel for the article, 'Holiday reading', on p. 74, from 'Journeys in print', published in *Financial Times*, 30 June 2001; Michael Legat for the 'Lucozade' text on p. 75, published in *Writing Magazine*, April–May 2001; for the Albert Einstein cartoon on p. 77, Gordon Wells for the script, Walter Howarth the artwork, published in *Writing Magazine*, June–July 2001, courtesy of *Kids Alive Magazine* © Salvation Army November 2000; for the listening material, 'Clean up the world' on p. 81, with kind permission of Taronga Zoo, Sydney and Clean up the World Pty Ltd. www.cleanup.com.au; for the article 'John Gould the bird man', on p. 85, by Tony Ward, published in *Antiques in NSW*, September–December 2002 © J Q Pty Ltd.; for the listening material, 'Architectural styles' on p. 87, adapted from *Handbook of Art* by Graham Hopwood, published by Science Press, Boden Books Pty Ltd.; Malcolm Gladwell for the article 'The naked face' on p. 94, first published in *The New Yorker*; for 'Reading Texts' on p. 106,

Professor David Crystal, *Cambridge Encyclopedia of Language*, published by 1997 © Cambridge University Press, reprinted with permission of the author and publisher; for the article 'F de Saussure' on p. 107, from *Saussure* by Johnathan Culler, published by HarperCollins 1985; for the article, 'Sign language in the brain', on p. 109, adapted from 'How does the human brain process language' by Gregory Hickock, Ursula Bellugi and Edward S. Klima. Copyright © June 2001 by Scientific American, Inc. All rights reserved.

The publishers are grateful to the following for permission to reproduce copyright photographs and material:

(Key: l = left, c = centre, r = right, t = top, b = bottom).

Action Images p. 13 (b); Alvey & Towers p. 63; Aquarius/Warner Bros. p. 72; aviation-images.com p. 103 (b); ©John Birdsall Photography p. 109 (b); Bruce Coleman Collection/Anders Blomqvist p. 87 (r); CORBIS/©Vince Streano p. 81; CORBIS Sygma/©Nobel Foundation p. 58; ©Christie's Images 2004 p. 85 (b); James Davies Photography p. 86 (t); Eye Ubiquitous/David A Burns p. 86 (bD), /Martin Shreeves p. 86 (bE); ©Financial Times p. 74 (b); GettyImages/Hulton Archive p. 67 (b); GettyImages/Imagebank/Adrian Weinbrecht p. 22 (t), /Kaz Mori p. 28 (t), /Anthony Johnson p. 36 (l), /Gen Nishino p. 42, /Yellow Dog Productions p. 50 (l), /White Packert pp. 55, 86 (bA), /Chris Alan Wilton p. 62, /G.D.T p. 69, /Ryan McVay p. 83 (l), /Theo Allofs p. 84 (t1), /Paul Souders p. 84 (t4), /Cousteau Society p. 84 (t6), /Andrea Pistolesi p. 90, /Ron Krisel p. 92 (bD), /Anne Rippy p. 92 (bB), /Ghislain & Marie David De Lossy p. 92 (bE), /Steve Satushek p. 98 (t); GettyImages/PhotoDisc Collection pp. 6 (tr), 53 (b); GettyImages/PhotoDisc/Andy Sotiriou p. 46 (t); GettyImages/Stone/John Kelly p. 14, /Ed Pritchard p. 36 (r), /Don Smetzer p. 49, /Stuart McClymont p. 54, /Paul S Conrath p. 68 (t), /Laurence Dutton p. 74 (t), /Kevin Schafer pp. 80, 84 (t5), /Darryl Torckler p. 84 (t3), /Deborah Jaffe p. 92 (bA), /Nicolas Bertrand p. 92 (bC); GettyImages/Taxi/Stuart Hughs p. 12 (b), /Rob Gage pp. 12 (t), 13 (t), 19, 20, 21, 27, 33, 39, 45, 48 (r), 51, 52, 53 (t), 59 (t), 60, 61, 67 (t), 73, 79, 85 (t), 91, 97, 103 (t), 109 (t), 110, 111, /Gary Buss p. 18, /Charles Benes p. 28 (c), /Eric Jacobson p. 40 (t), /Michael Krasowitz p. 83 (m), /Antonio Mo p. 83 (r), /Jonathan and Angela p. 84 (t2), /Christian Michaels p. 92 (t), /Manfred Rutz p. 94, /Peter Adams p. 104; Impact/©Caroline Penn p. 59 (b), /©Brian Rybolt p. 86 (bB); Network Photographers pp. 31, 84 (bl); PA Photos/ABACA p. 68 (b); Photofusion/©Christa Stadtler p. 46 (b), /©Steve Morgan p. 65, /©John Phillips p. 77 (tl), /©Ute Klaphake p. 77 (tr); Pictorial Press p. 70; Popperfoto/Reuters p. 77 (b); Rex Features/©Ray Tang p. 84 (br); Science Photo Library/Julian Baum & David Angus p. 29, /Phil Jude p. 34, /Peter Menzel p. 98 (b); 'Mission To Saturn', by David M Harland. A Springer-Praxis cover courtesy of Praxis Publishing Ltd, designed by Jim Wilkie, Havant, Hants p. 10; Still Pictures pp. 44, 84 (b); ©TravelInk/Colin Marshall p. 24, /Derek Allan p. 86 (bC), /Dennis Stone p. 87 (l); John Walmsley pp. 48 (l), 50 (r).

The following photographs were taken on commission for CUP by Trevor Clifford:

pp. 6 (m), 16, 17, 22 (b), 40 (b), 78, 88, 102.

Picture research by Hilary Fletcher.